ABANDONMENT TO
ACCEPTANCE

A Hero's Journey to Self-Love

By Fran Wilson

Published by Women's Biz Global
New South Wales, Australia
womensbizglobal.com

Book Layout © 2024 womensbizglobal.com

ABANDONMENT TO ACCEPTANCE / Fran Wilson-- 1st ed.
978-1-922969-21-7

womensbizglobal.com

CONTENTS

INRODUCTION

A HERO'S JOURNEY TO SELF-LOVE

Disclaimer
This book contains references to domestic violence. While the author has taken great lengths to ensure the subject matter is dealt with in a compassionate, informed, and respectful manner, it may be triggering for some readers, therefore discretion is advised. This book is not intended as a substitute for professional advice; therefore, we encourage readers to seek support to access domestic support services.

One morning back in February 2023, I had an epiphany moment. For some reason, a little voice in my head, with so much motivation and passion shouted, "Fran you have got to write a book around the topic of overcoming the fear of rejection". I was a bit taken aback by this at first. But I thought about it and I said to myself, "Yes, I can do that…I will do exactly that…I'll publish my first book and get my message and story out there, so I can empower people around the world".

Rejection and the fear of being rejected are one of the most distressing emotional states that we face as human beings. Emotional rejection is a feeling we experience when we don't get what we desire and face situations we cannot control. It is about acceptance, or in this case, not being accepted for who we are. It is commonly experienced in a quest for emotional relations, such as in an intimate relationship, in social and group settings, or in a professional career capacity.

Social rejection and this fear of rejection occur when an individual is deliberately excluded from a social relationship or social interaction. This includes interpersonal rejection (or peer rejection), romantic rejection and abandonment. It can manifest itself as an intense dread of being rejected or being abandoned by friends, family, colleagues, or partners. Furthermore, rejection can be active, in ways such as bullying, teasing, or ridiculing. It can also be passive, by ignoring a person, giving the "silent treatment", or being cold with them.

The experience of being rejected is subjective, and I personally believe that both active and passive rejection are forms of mental and emotional bullying that no one deserves.

The experience of rejection can lead to a number of adverse psychological consequences such as a sudden drop in confidence, loneliness, low self-esteem, low self-worth, depression and a victim mindset. The fear of rejection appears as disappointment, sadness, depression, anxiety, aggression, phobic behaviour, stalking the person doing the rejecting, and even suicidal thoughts or actions. It can also lead to feelings of insecurity and a heightened sensitivity to future rejection.

As people, we are programmed to expect rejection no matter what situation we're in, where we are, or who we're with. The causes of the fear of rejection ranges from such things as having a physical condition that makes a person feel unattractive in society to being rejected as a child, or having been abandoned, unloved, or unwanted in a toxic relationship. Another reason may be from a traumatic experience of rejection that has long-term emotional effects. It can be an accumulation of multiple negative experiences.

Fear of rejection can lead to co-dependency, clingy, obsessive, jealous, or angry behaviour in relationships. It can drive others away…more often than not, the people we love and care about the most. In general, fear of rejection can result in a very damaging pattern of emotion and behaviour that can cause real hurt, pain and suffering in relationships and destroy our happiness in life. It takes control of our life and prevents us from being our true authentic self. We become numb and hollow inside, and we prevent ourselves from being who we were born to be.

I wrote this book, as a lot of what I have mentioned, I have experienced myself. These personal experiences came from abandonment by family members, rejection in my engineering career, as well as many rejections in my love life. Now is the time I get to give myself permission to share my story. My untold story, where I express how I feel about these negative and traumatic experiences, what I did to overcome my forty years of hurt and this fear of rejection that was preventing me from living the life I was born to live.

We all want to feel accepted and loved by our family, friends and peers. But for many of us, the fear of rejection or abandonment can be so strong that it prevents us from even trying to make those connections. Fear of rejection is a very real phenomenon that affects millions of people around the world.

The purpose of this book is to help you understand the root causes of your fear, so you can work towards overcoming it and develop more fulfilling relationships with people around you.

It explores different aspects of rejection, such as why we feel the need for acceptance from others, how we create expectations about what people should do for us in order to gain approval, and understanding why some people are more prone to feeling rejected than others. Through self-reflection exercises and psychological insights, it hopefully provides you with strategies to overcome the fear of rejection or abandonment, so you can live a happier life filled with meaningful connections, instead of loneliness and despair.

If you are living your life in this way, locked in a vicious cycle of fear of rejection and want to have the breakthrough to overcome this pain and suffering, I want this book to empower and inspire you, so that you too get to face your rejection and abandonment demons head on, and transcend beyond this fear of rejection. This in turn will allow you to live your life on your terms, and make you feel unstoppable, giving you the feeling of complete personal freedom.

"I am committed to creating a world of freedom, love, peace, connection, and abundance." - Fran Wilson

CHAPTER ONE

REJECTION WELCOMES ME

"Dad, I'm here... where are you?"

For me, life did not start off the way it should have been. My introduction into the world was very complicated.

You see, my mother, Annie, was in a very toxic and abusive relationship. She met a man named Mark, an electrician by trade, who had emigrated from French Guiana, South America, with his father in the 1970's.

It appeared to be love at first sight between Annie and Mark. They had a baby girl, my sister Dee, in 1978. Due to the nature of their relationship, my father pushed my mother so far over the edge, she ended up taking an overdose. He was so abusive, he even pushed her down the stairs, when she was pregnant again. How she survived that horrific ordeal, I have no idea. Unfortunately, however, she lost the baby. This was now the point where social services intervened as it had gotten too much for my mother to handle.

Dee was put into care when she was three years old and was eventually adopted into a different family in the north of England. My mother fell pregnant again in 1982. I have no idea why she kept going back to Mark, but she did. This time, she was pregnant with me. My mother lived on a high-level floor in a high-rise block of flats in Luton, in England. One day, when social services were visiting the property, my dad appeared to be very angry and full of rage towards my mother, and inexplicably said something along the lines of, "I want to throw her over the balcony". This immediately raised red flags and alarm bells and of course, social services had to escalate the need to ensure she was safe to not only give my mother the protection she needed, but also the protection I needed, as an unborn child.

It was the first of March, 1983, a Tuesday morning. The world was about to get a very special delivery…Yes, me. At 5:35am, my mother gave birth in the hospital. I weighed 6lb 6oz and I was christened Jason Connaughton. Everything appeared to be normal, and I was a gorgeous, healthy baby. However, everything wasn't what it should have been.

Not knowing…sure how could I, but the truth was that I was never going home with my mother that day. She was made aware of the situation by social services in that they were there to take me away and put me into foster care. It was completely devastating for her. She felt empty inside, and there was nothing that she could do for me, other than to let me go. She loved me so much and she was heartbroken, only having a few hours with me before I was taken away from her forever.

I still don't know much about my father, and I have never met him, but I believe he was in another relationship at the same time and had multiple children by the time he had met my mother. He was not there for me in the hospital the day I was born. He was nowhere to be seen and seemingly did not care about me at all. He does not care about me to this very day.

Instead, social services were there at the hospital waiting to take me away from my mother on the day I was born. I cannot imagine what it must have been like for my mother all on her own that day. She must have been traumatised, upset and heartbroken, knowing her child, who was only a few hours old, was being taken away from her. It must have been devastating. Not only that, but this was the second time her child was taken away from her. Social services gave my mother the respect and dignity she deserved, by allowing her to say goodbye to me that Tuesday afternoon. I imagine this was the hardest thing she's ever had to do.

So, from day one, I experienced rejection…not from my mother, but because of the difficult and stressful situation she was in. It was not her fault. Rejection truly did welcome me into the world. I clearly did not have any control or have a say in the matter, but this was soon to be the start of a long and difficult path for me. That afternoon of the day I was born, I left the hospital with social services, instead of my mother. They made sure I was looked after, and I was immediately put into foster care. I'm not going to go into the details about my adoption process, but I reconnected with my biological mother, thirty-four years later, which was incredible. I wanted to give my mother the opportunity to share her story about what happened that day.

Having now heard and understood what had happened from my mother's perspective, it is great to hear that I was always loved by her. She never stopped thinking of me. As I said, she did not want to let go of me. To date, I have not been given the opportunity to hear my father's perspective. He was not there for me the day I was born. He was nowhere to be seen. I do not understand why a parent would not be there at the birth of their child. To me, this is not love…far from it.

Abusing my mother and putting her through so much pain and suffering - this is the opposite of love. My father abandoned and rejected me before even meeting me. Why would a father reject their newborn child? Only he can answer that question.

Over forty years later and I still have no urgency or desire to ever meet him. I believe there may be too much anger and resentment there. I am finding it difficult to come to terms with it. Who knows, maybe it might give me closure on the matter, even if I meet him just once and give him the opportunity to explain himself…Maybe.

It was not long before I was truly loved and welcomed into a family. A young married couple from London, Mr and Mrs Wilson, submitted an application to adopt me. They had already adopted three other children from three other families, and they wanted one more, and guess what, I was the chosen one!

I was eventually adopted into the Wilson family in December 1983, nine months after I was born. This is why I have an adoption day on the 15th of December every year. I describe it as being a celebration of when I was officially loved and welcomed into the world. I've always seen it as a second birthday. My siblings have the same thing, and we still celebrate this today, acknowledging each other's adoption day. It's a day I do not feel rejected, but rather, I feel a sense of being welcomed into this unique loving family.

My name was changed from Jason to Francis because Mr and Mrs Wilson wanted to name me after the adoption agency in Milton Keynes, where my adoption was processed. This agency was called 'St. Francis' Children's Society'.

Growing up, I always knew that I was adopted. This has been a good thing, as it's very respectful and it's nice to see my parents were open and transparent about this. They did not want to hide anything from me or my siblings. All they wanted was to love and protect us all. However, it didn't all go according to plan.

New Dad, where are you going?

In 1996, when I was thirteen years old, the dynamics of our family changed forever. You see, my adopted father (dad) Mr Wilson, worked away a lot of the time. My adopted mother (mum) Sandra was also working with clients as a marriage therapist. So, we were really a normal family. Nothing unusual. Just a typical family working hard just to get by.

It was in October when everything changed. My dad had been on a business trip to South Africa for a few days. Everything seemed normal, until one day, around Halloween, our parents asked us all to sit down together as they had a big announcement to make. Immediately my heart started to race. I knew something was wrong. In fact, I remember feeling quite scared, as we never did this kind of thing as a family. So we all sat down in the room at the back of the house in Dublin. I remember sitting in the corner, worried and curious about what was about to happen.

My dad announced that he had met another woman on his recent business trip to South Africa and that he was planning on moving out there straight away to be with her. All of our hearts broke as this signalled the end of our happy family. I guess I did not know how to process it, or even how mum was feeling. We were all simply shocked that we were no longer going to have dad in our lives. Obviously, he had the conversation with mum first, who was clearly heartbroken and devastated.

To me, it felt like a nightmare, one that I knew I was going to wake up from soon. I could not understand what was happening. I couldn't process this information. It felt like my world was collapsing and our family was falling apart.

We all had so many questions…the obvious one…Why? How could you do this to us?

This was my first real-life experience of abandonment. My adopted father walking out on me…on us. I have now had two fathers abandon me. I was only 13 years old at this point. Somehow, our family stayed strong, and we supported each other as best we could. I don't know how my mum did what she did to look after the four of us. I could write another book about her alone. She is an incredible human being and an angel who kept us all going, believed in us and did what she could to protect us all. I would not be where I am today without her. She has been my beacon of light and the source of my strength and energy.

I was affected by this scenario quite badly. I remember how I used to smoke cigarettes in my social circle and with my siblings to numb the pain. Yes, I smoked when I was 13 years old. I'll never forget Christmas 1996, as that was definitely the worst Christmas of my life. I suffered from cigarette-related bronchitis for about two weeks and mum had to look after me on her own. She took me to the doctor and got all the medication that I needed. I was in such a bad way, and I believe a lot of it was down to dealing with the trauma of losing my dad to another woman. I may never know for certain, but that experience of my dad leaving may have played a big part in how my mind and body reacted to that shocking news. How do you deal with that at the age of 13 years old, let alone any age?

Sticks and stones may break my bones…

But the rejection didn't end there around this period of my life.

Being a teenager and growing up can be a difficult experience for many of us, and feeling accepted by those around us is often a major concern and challenge. Unfortunately, there are too many stories about children being rejected or even bullied in school due to their background or skin colour. Racism and discrimination still exist in our society today, and it's heartbreaking to think that young people have to deal with such hatred because of who they are.

We all want to feel worthy and feel like we belong in society; however, when faced with the fear of rejection from peers or teachers, it can make it hard for students to express themselves without worrying about how they will be judged. This fear of not being accepted can lead to low self-esteem which then impacts other areas of life including academics and relationships.

Growing up in a white community as a mixed-race child, I never felt completely accepted. As a mixed-race person, people would often throw racist comments at me on the streets. I was always called the "N" word, whether it was playing in the schoolyard, or out in the public parks, it was always there in front of me. It just became part of my life. I told myself to accept these hurtful comments, as there was nothing I could do. But it was frustrating and made me feel like an outcast – someone who didn't belong anywhere.

At school, I was regularly bullied for being different. People would whisper behind my back or laugh in my face when I passed by. They would throw things at me in the classroom. It instilled a deep fear in me of rejection and feeling unwelcome wherever I went. Despite trying my best to fit in, these experiences made it difficult for me to make real connections with others.

I even remember hearing these comments in nightclubs when I was around eighteen years of age.

It's important to stand up against racism and prejudice and create inclusive communities where everyone feels accepted regardless of race, gender identity, sexual orientation, or any other factor. I accept everyone for who they are, and that's exactly what I want of me. For everyone to accept me for who I am. Not for what I do, or how much is in my bank, but for the great gift that I bring to the world... Freedom, Peace, Love, Connection, and Abundance...We all matter.

CHAPTER TWO

WHY DO I FEEL ALONE IN A BUSY WORLD?

I have never really thought of my adoption in detail until now, writing this book. I have always known that I was adopted…as long as I can remember. In fact, all four children in my family were adopted and we always knew.

Our adopted parents never wanted to keep that a secret from us or tell us at a certain time or age. I must admit, I admire them for their courage and bravery in telling us at all. It couldn't have been easy for them. After forty years, I asked my mum about this, as I wanted to understand it from her perspective.

Here is what she told me…

Me, through the eyes of my mother.

"When people tell me how lucky my children are I always reply, 'No, I am the lucky one; we are, all of us, just so blessed to have found each other.'

My journey with adoption began when I was around seven. One day in school after the morning break there was a scream of anger from the back of the class and a voice cried out," I hate you, you're not my mother". The girl at the back of the class had been told in the playground by a friend that her mother, who was the teacher, had adopted her.

I didn't understand at the time, but the moment always stayed with me and when I discovered I was unable to have children, the experience all those years before took on greater importance. Remembering the outrage of my school friend when she was told her mother hadn't given birth to her, I wondered, 'how on earth do you tell your child they are adopted and when do you tell them?' We decided to make the day we adopted each of our children a special day, like a birthday with presents and cake. We started this in the first year they were adopted, and they gradually came to understand the word without major trauma, or so it seemed. Their schoolteachers loved the idea and gave no homework on that day, so being adopted was seen as something very positive by their peers.

As I grew with my children and studied psychology, I began to realise that my school friend had screamed in rage not because she didn't like or love her adoptive mother, but because she was overwhelmed with a sense of rejection by her birth mother. Just imagine the difference for an embryo in a womb where a pregnancy is welcomed and celebrated with joy and anticipation, then compare it with one that is feared, rejected and unwanted. Imagine the different birth experience of a baby that is welcomed, loved and cherished on arrival, to the one where the baby is removed from mother, the bond broken, and the child thrust into the unknown.

I believe many adopted children and adults carry a deep and lasting sense of rejection, which colours the greater lives. Feelings of rejection are accompanied by feelings of anger, grief and loss, which in turn damages their sense of self-esteem. The unconscious voice of, 'there must be something wrong with me for my birth parents to give me away', prevails until made conscious in later life. Of course, this separation trauma is mediated by adoptive parents, but can never be healed by them.

In my own situation, I believe I have probably overcompensated for this sense of rejection, especially after my husband left us out of the blue when my children were only in their teens. I felt so deeply my own loss and here were my four adopted children, losing yet another parent. No parent is perfect, birth parent or adoptive parent. No matter how hard we try to make our children's lives happy, productive and fulfilled, we will never get it all right. We are human. Parenthood is a lifetime journey of love and sharing and learning together.

Raising my adopted children has been the single most amazing and rewarding thing that has ever happened in my life.

Back over to you 'Blossom'.

Is love and loss a numbers game?

Thanks, blossom, for those lovely words...'Blossom' is the nickname we have for each other.

Sadly, proudly, my story is just one of many. Whilst scrolling the internet for statistics and facts around adoption, I stumbled on some very powerful and relatable words. These words have become the epitome of my existence; they have held me back, caused me pain, inflicted yet more rejection, and finally set me free.

According to the U.S. Department of Health and Human Services Administration [AH1] for Children and Families Administration on Children, Youth and Families Children's Bureau, members of the adoption constellation may experience any number of the following seven core issues related to adoption:

1. Loss
2. Rejection
3. Grief

4. Shame and Guilt
5. Identity
6. Intimacy
7. Mastery and control.

I'm not from the U.S, but I'm sure this is universal, no matter where you live. However, I won't go into too much detail on these, as different people experience a combination of these to varying degrees. For example, my biological mother, Annie, will have a complete set of experiences to me. However, I want to share this from a male perspective. As a man, I believe other men who have been through or are going through a similar experience, need to hear this. I feel I never had anyone to talk to about this when I was growing up. Or maybe I didn't feel ready to speak about it. Therefore, I want to create a safe-space here and now, where men can be comforted by my story, knowing that it wasn't their fault, and they're not alone.

The power in a name

Perhaps you also have a different name. Perhaps your name reflects the adoration of your new 'parents'. Perhaps you have been named after someone famous and inspirational. Perhaps your name will become your legacy for your people further down the line. But before we seek solace in what we gained from adoption, let's look a little closer at what we may have lost along the way.

In terms of **'loss'**, I lost my birth family, including siblings, grandparents, aunts and uncles. I lost a cultural and societal connection. I always look back and think, 'what if I was never adopted? What would my life look like growing up on the streets of Luton, just outside London, instead of in the Irish countryside?' It's literally a sliding door moment. Don't think I never wanted to be with my adopted family. No, not at all. I am so very grateful for the upbringing I had. I wouldn't change it. However, losing biological parents is never easy. How do you process that information, that loss?

For me, because I was blessed with 'new' parents, it was never a big issue. It's not as if I was born into this world and witnessed all of the abuse in that toxic relationship or was a part of the legal case between my biological parents. That would have been a completely different situation and a different set of feelings for me. Thankfully, I did not have to go through that traumatic experience. So, I guess instead of losing, I gained a new family, a loving family, and three amazing, adopted siblings.

In terms of **'rejection'**, I believe that I was in a fighting battle before my life even began. I believe this part of my life is where all the rejection feelings originated. I did feel rejected, particularly by my biological father. I had so many questions to ask. Even to this day, I still haven't got the answers I want and will probably never get them. Why was he so aggressive towards my mother? Why was he not there for me at the hospital the day I was born? Why did he not care about me and love me? It wasn't my fault what was going on. I didn't deserve that. I needed both of my parents there loving me, regardless of their differences. I needed them both at the hospital holding me, watching my first smile, changing my first nappy. But instead, social services were there to protect me. Was I not good enough? Was I not worthy of being loved? I believe this was a massive sub-conscious scar that I have been carrying around with me my whole life.

'Grief' is an interesting one for me, as I don't feel I have been consciously grieving my whole life, but maybe subconsciously I have. I've never felt a sense of pain from this experience in my life.

This is why the subconscious mind is so dominant in our thoughts and emotions. Maybe I chose to block out this grief, this pain and suffering of not being good enough for a family in Luton. As far as I was concerned, I had simply accepted what had happened to me. Adoption is just a part of life, isn't it?

They say that **'shame and guilt'** about adoption or being adopted may worsen feelings of grief. The shame of being involved in adoption may again be subconscious for me. Shame and guilt associated with my adoption more than likely affected my self-esteem, discouraged me from thinking positively about myself, and limited me from loving and receiving love from others. Yes, I can definitely relate to this. I feel ashamed because my biological parents were unable to raise me themselves, maybe not unable to, but chose not to. Although my mother was prepared to love me and care for me, the situation had gone so far that it was affecting her own mental health and had pushed her over the limit. My father was not interested in me at all. I have never felt loved by him, and I probably never will. He had given up on me before I was even born. A lack of self-love is something that I'm fully aware of now, which is why this is number one for me…Love me, it's time to love Fran Wilson.

Now for me, **'identity'** is a big one. I have experienced adoption-related identity issues throughout my life, especially around milestones such as birthdays. I do see my identity as incomplete, unsteady, or contradictory. I have said many times that I have lost my identity…Did I ever have one? When I was born, I was christened Jason Stephen Connaughton, but when I was adopted, my name was changed to Francis Wilson. So, who am I? I feel like Fran, but who really is Fran? I only discovered in my fortieth year that I am a powerful, authentic, loving leader, and I stand for growth, freedom, and transformation. This is who I truly believe I am.

I think for me **'intimacy'** is an interesting one...people would associate attachment issues of trying to avoid experiencing a new loss by keeping an emotional distance from or not committing to someone else. Whereas in my case, I hate the idea of not being around people, but more importantly, the thought of losing someone whilst in an intimate relationship. Especially someone I adore and love. For instance, every partner I have had in a long-term relationship has walked out on me. I always wanted to feel close to them and never wanted any of them to leave me. I guess I needed the intimacy...I wanted to feel secure and looked after by my partner. However, I never truly felt that. So, for me, I craved intimacy. Maybe it's a male thing, or maybe it's simply the side effects of other forms of abandonment in my life. My desire was to feel loved...feel wanted, feel special and adored by someone else. I knew I didn't receive that when I was born. I must have longed for it on my journey in life. However, I have recently discovered that I have a co-dependency issue and that I had been searching for my happiness through other people.

For me, **'Mastery and Control'** was not a big concern. Because I was adopted at such a young age, I would not have been involved in the decisions that led to the adoption. These decisions were made by other people. However, I do want to be in control of my life and one strategy that I use is building resilience. Resilience is the ability to adapt or cope in a positive way to adversity, including trauma, tragedy, threats and significant stress, which I certainly have experienced. I believe because I was adopted, resilience is in my DNA. Maybe it was to prove a point to myself and the world. Resilience helps me thrive despite the accompanying, loss, grief, rejection, and intimacy issues I have experienced in my life.

If you are flooded by these words, take this as your permission slip to:

Surrender to the loss
Acknowledge your past
Embrace your worth
Feel each feeling
And focus on your future. Because that part hasn't happened yet.

Before I move onto the next chapter, where I talk about becoming a father myself after adoption, I want to dig a bit deeper into my adoption journey. I have been fortunate to get my hands on a lot of the paperwork from my foster mother, as well as the court proceedings, and I thought it would be good to include some of these manuscripts in this book.

Letters from 1983

When I first read the collection of letters from the local councils, courthouses, and my foster mother written during my adoption process, I felt a greater understanding of my early days in life. I didn't feel anger, abandonment or rejection; I felt fascinated. I know, this may sound the opposite to what you may assume about a book about rejection, but really, I felt pure relief at how well I was treated.

In these beautiful snippets plucked from my past, you will read my journey and hopefully believe your worth on this little planet.

Letter #1 – From Foster Mother to Mr and Mrs Wilson dated 18th April 1983.

"I find Jason a dear little baby with a gentle nature who takes a solemn interest in what is going on around him. He seems to need personal contact and really likes being nursed and talked to. He started talking at four weeks old and first smiled two weeks later.

He has just started having five feeds a day. I let him wake himself for the first one, which is about 6:30-7am. He is then fed approximately every four hours. I occasionally have to wake him. After the 3:30pm feed he has his crying time. He starts about one and a half hours after his feed and is unhappy and restless until the next feed, which I give him after three hours about 6-6:30pm. He usually settles after this feed and I always have to wake him for the fifth feed at about 11-11:30pm.

Using SMA gold top and a medium hole teat, I make him a 5oz feed, as I have just started giving him this amount he doesn't always finish it. I wind him halfway through, as well as at the end.

On most occasions he stays up about ¾ hour after his bottle and spends the time being nursed, playing with, sitting in the baby relax chair and having a kick with his nappy off – usually on my knee, as he is not very happy on the floor.

At changing times, I have found that after cleansing with baby lotion and covering of Morhulin cream is all that has been necessary to keep him free from nappy rash.

When it is time for bed he is used to being wrapped in a shawl and put down on alternate sides to sleep. If he is awake when I go to bed, I have found he settles much better if I leave the light on.

Date	Age	Weight
1ˢᵗ March 1983	New Born	6lb 6oz
15ᵗʰ March 1983	2 weeks old	6lb 14 ½oz
22ⁿᵈ March 1983	3 weeks old	7lb 4 ¾oz
29ᵗʰ March 1983	4 weeks old	7lb 12 ¾oz
4ᵗʰ April 1983	5 weeks old	8lb 2 ¾oz
11ᵗʰ April 1983	6 weeks old	8lb 10oz
18ᵗʰ April 1983	7 weeks old	7lb 0 ¼oz

These are his naked weights."

Letter #2 – From Buckinghamshire County Council Social Worker to Mr and Mrs Wilson dated 29th April 1983.

"Dear Mr and Mrs Wilson,

Thank you for your letter of 19th April informing us of the placement of Jason Stephen Connaughton with your family.

I would like to meet you and the baby on Monday 9th May at approximately 6.45pm. If that is inconvenient, please let me know.
I look forward to seeing you then.

Yours sincerely"

CHAPTER THREE

WHY DO I HURT SO MUCH?

Is this what love feels like?

One of the most important and life-changing experiences was now about to happen to me. I was about to embark on a journey of my first love. This happened when I was still at home with my incredible, loving and supportive mum. I was studying Mechanical Engineering in the Institute of Technology, Tallaght (ITT), in Dublin, Ireland. This course was three years and at the end of 2003, I was awarded a Diploma.

I was always hard-working and fully committed to putting in the effort to achieve the best results. I'll never forget when I buddied up with two of my closest friends while on this course. We would always do assignments and study together at each other's houses. When it came to exam time, our efforts had paid off. All three of us would get A's and B's across the board. It was such a great feeling.

This was also around the time I turned 18. I was finally considered an adult and had the freedom to go out, socialise with my friends and enjoy a few drinks. Growing up, I always had a couple of best friends, the type of friends who were always there for me. I'm still close to them today. One of my best friends is Joe. Joe and I were inseparable growing up. We did everything together.

It was only when we both turned 18, we decided to go out at the weekends to nightclubs and watch our favourite DJs play. We were very big into this at the time and even bought the full set of DJ equipment to experiment with in our bedrooms (Technic 1210s).

It was on a night out in March 2003, when I connected with a lovely girl named Charlie. Long story short, myself and Charlie eventually started dating and before we knew it, we were in a relationship. It was very exciting for me as this became my first serious relationship. I was now a responsible adult, and I had my duty to look after Charlie and make sure she was happy. My best friend, Joe, was dating Charlie's best friend. The four of us would always hang out together. We even went on a two-week holiday together to Corfu.

It would have been sometime around May or June in 2003, and I don't know how the conversation started, but one day when I was studying with my friends, we discussed the opportunity about what we would do once we had completed our Diploma in Tallaght, Dublin. Why not all move over to the UK together, so we could build a career in the motorsport and automotive industry? I know I was super excited by this, and I was already starting to plan it in my head.

Being a huge motorsport fan, it just made sense to me. I would always watch Formula 1 whenever it was on television (I still do today!) and used to think how amazing it would be if I was one of those mechanics you see in the pit lane, changing the tyres in under two seconds for Lewis Hamilton. Or if I was one of the race engineers sitting up on the pitwall in front of all those screens, looking at the data from the car and speaking directly to Lewis himself. What a dream come true that would be. Once this idea came into my head, I could not shake it off. I was so excited. Of course, me being me, I went off and did some research. I looked at where I could study automotive and motorsport and qualify with a Bachelor's Degree. Finally, I found somewhere…Oxford.

After a few weeks of doing some research, myself and one of my friends decided to take that leap of faith and relocate to Oxford, live in student halls of accommodation, and pursue our dream to become the next top Formula 1 engineer.

I'll never forget applying for a place at Oxford Brookes University through the clearing system. Clearing is the system employed by UCAS (Universities and Colleges Admissions Service) and UK universities at the end of the academic year to fill course places that haven't been taken. It allows universities to fill spaces on courses that aren't yet full, while students without offers are given a second chance to pursue their higher education aspirations. In my case, it was a last-minute dream.

My family could not believe me when I told them in August 2003 that I was moving to the UK the following month, to start the next academic year in Automotive Engineering. My mum genuinely did not believe I would go ahead and actually move to the UK. It was so ambitious, and nothing anyone in our family had done before, but I was serious.

You're probably thinking, how does this relate to my first love rejection? You see, the plan was for me to go over to the UK on my own, as Charlie was busy studying in Dublin, herself. She was very passionate about dentistry and was learning to become a dental nurse. So, there was never any plan for us both to move to the UK together. I never wanted to put that pressure on her. To be honest, I think my plan deep down was to stay over there in the UK, as I was so focused on getting the qualification, then planned to review the situation with Charlie after that.

When I moved to the UK from Dublin in September 2003, I was 20 years old and filled with an array of emotions – excitement for the new adventure that awaited me and a sense of loneliness and fear for being in a new environment all on my own, without Charlie. Little did I know, however, that not only would this be a journey filled with exciting experiences and newfound friendships, but also one that would challenge and test my resilience, as I confronted one of life's most difficult realities – rejection.

Maybe I didn't appreciate what I had with my first love. We had grown close over the months leading up to my departure, but there were mixed feelings in the air, as we both knew our relationship would never be the same again when we said goodbye. Despite our doubts and worries, we held each other tight and promised each other that no matter how hard it may be to stay together over a long distance, we would fight for our love.

I arrived in the great city of Oxford full of optimism and expectation; ready to take on the world. My mum and other family members helped me get settled into the new place. It was such a stressful time, as we had to buy everything, I needed for my studio apartment in the student halls of residence. I'll always remember the day when they left me on my own. I had never felt so lonely and felt terrified. Even though my friend was not far away in different student halls nearby, I honestly did not think I could stay. I remember being very emotional every day for weeks, calling my mum saying, *"I can't do this"*. Somehow, I found the strength within me due to the support from my family, to keep going and never give up. Charlie was also very supportive and kept me optimistic.

One of the highlights for me was when Charlie booked a surprise trip over to me for my 21st birthday. My newly formed uni friends were communicating with Charlie (as Charlie had been visiting only a few weeks earlier, and they swapped phone numbers). They had it all planned. I had no idea. It was only when we were in the onsite student nightclub, when I was on the dancefloor. All of a sudden, I had my eyes covered and a few seconds later, I received a kiss on my lips. I was completely confused. However, when I opened my eyes, I could not believe it. Charlie was there standing in front of me smiling. I was literally lost for words. I was so happy, and a little drunk of course! It was an amazing night and birthday weekend.

I went from Ecstasy to Agony

However, this dream was soon to come crashing down. Within my second year of starting university life abroad - despite our best efforts - Charlie had decided that she no longer wanted to be in a relationship with me. The strain of being in a long-distance relationship had ultimately become too much for her. I'll never forget when I was in her house, back in Dublin on September 11th, 2004, and I could see she wanted to end the relationship. She had made up her mind and nothing I said would change her mind. I was on my knees begging her not to leave me. I was so broken. I did not want to lose what we had. I loved her.

I don't know why she did what she did, following this heartbreaking conversation, but a few days later, when I was out in town with my friend having a good night out, Charlie found out from her best friend where we were having a few drinks. Much to my horror, she walked into the same place with another man. My heart was ripped apart when I saw this. I felt sick. I was so hurt, upset and betrayed. This was my first love rejection moment, and it was like she wanted to avenge me for some reason. I knew this was the end of our relationship, but I did not know how to handle it. I was in pain. I wanted to give up on everything and I simply found the pain unbearable. I was not prepared to experience a relationship failure…A rejection from the person I loved and who said they loved me. I had no coping mechanism for this. Maybe it was because I was too naive and never expected it to happen to me.

Although deeply saddened by what had happened between us, after many years of reflection, I can now look back on those moments with lightness, rather than darkness. In hindsight, the crushing sense of abandonment brought clarity into understanding myself better and taught me valuable lessons about relationships and resilience, which have served me well since then. Charlie has now married and had children with someone else. I have come to terms with this and have accepted that this is what life is all about.

CHAPTER FOUR

IS THIS IT… IS THIS LIFE?

Life seemed to be going by so well for me with everything just flowing smoothly. It was the start of 2009, and I was in this amazing job as a Transmission and Driveline Test Engineer for the global brand, Jaguar Land Rover. I was also in a new relationship with a girl called Jen, from London. We met in April 2008, and we had just moved in together in a rented property in Banbury the following January. So only a few months after meeting each other for the first time. I was in love, had a great job, and my health was fine. Everything was perfect.

"Fran, we're having a baby!"

I was just twenty-six years old, and still trying to find my feet in the world. Then one day, I heard four words that would change my life forever: "Fran, we're having a baby". Trust me, becoming a father as an adoptee was perhaps the most surreal, confronting, and magical experience I've ever felt. I had not long been with my partner at the time, and we had just moved into a rented accommodation together, eight months after meeting for the first time.

Finding out about our pregnancy was a huge shock for me. I mean, why wouldn't it be? I was in a new relationship, still navigating my own feelings as an adopted child, crafting my career, and discovering how to be an adult myself. However, if there is one thing I am, it's loyal. I'm many more things, but without loyalty, I believe the world is a grey, lonely and dismal place.

The impact the news had on me was so big that my mind could not process it at the time. I could not compute that I was about to be a father, that I was about to be a responsible adult. Because I didn't know how to handle this, I thought of every scenario in my head. Deep down, I knew there was only one option and that was to keep our new baby, but it was the fact that I was so terrified about it, my mind started playing games. I thought about the possibility of my partner having an abortion, knowing that was the last thing I wanted. I thought about adoption, and then I remembered how I came into the world. I didn't want the same for our baby. I couldn't even begin to start thinking about that scenario. Basically, there was no other option but to have this baby and love it with all my heart, and to be the best parent possible that it deserved.

I was not recession-proof

My only concern at the time was the impact of the financial crisis. Because I was contracting through an agency, I was very nervous about the stability of my job. I was anxious about the thought of having to provide for my pregnant partner in such an unstable economy. How was I to do that? I saw a wave of people lose their jobs just before Christmas, which was heartbreaking to watch. Somehow, I survived, but that was not the end of the redundancies. My life was now put on hold. I was left in suspense and my fate was left in the hands of a global company who had the power to decide whether I could keep a roof over our heads and put food on the table, or not.

I'll never forget that day in April 2009 when my manager walked into the test rig office. He came straight over to my desk. Somehow, I knew what he was about to tell me. My fate was sealed, and he told me that sadly, he had no choice but to serve me the standard four weeks' notice. He admitted he did not want to do it but had to. His hands were tied, and a small consolation was that he was just as upset as I was…well maybe not quite as upset.

I didn't know how to break the news to my partner, and I felt like I'd let her down. It's hard to describe the feeling of what it was like to lose a job, while trying to look after my pregnant partner. It felt like I had the weight of the world on my shoulders. I kept saying to myself, *"Why was I let go? I did nothing wrong? It's so unfair."*

Not only did I lose my job, but I also lost the connections and friends that I had made while working at the global company. One of my friends in the team was always so nice to me and I remembered how I would always ask him how to operate the complex transmission test rigs. He always had time to show me how to set up and commission the control system. I respected him so much for this, as I was very passionate about building my skills and knowledge in using these systems.

In fact, we grew so close that we started doing things together outside of work. He became my best friend and took me on great days out. He was a Birmingham City football fan and he was a season ticket holder. He would invite me to some of the games and get me tickets so I could attend. I would meet him at a pub in Birmingham, not far from the football stadium, and we would have a few beers together, with some of his close friends.

He also used to take me fishing and invited me out for lunch with his family as well, which was amazing. It was so nice, and I actually felt wanted and included by him, even though I was soon to be leaving the department, which was so tough to face.

My stress and anxiety levels were through the roof. I was doing my best to pay the bills, especially the rent. It got to a point very quickly where I had no choice but to claim rental benefits. We were on a six-month contract and from what I remember, we were struggling to keep up with the rental payments. We had no other option but to hand in our tenancy notice. We could not afford to live there any longer.

Becoming an overnight adult

So, what myself and Jen did was to temporarily move in with Jen's parents in Merstham, South London. This was a lifesaver, as we had no income at this point. I'm sure you can relate to this if you've suffered a job loss. It's one of the worst experiences you can face. It truly is devastating. It lowers your confidence and makes you feel like you are not valued at all in a company - a company you had dedicated and sacrificed so much for. Instead, you end up being treated like a number and that is exactly how I felt…a number in the system…a broken system. I was so naive at the time and I didn't think anything of it. I simply accepted that was the way the corporate world operated. Society had taught me no different up until this point, so I just went with it, accepted it and didn't even consider doing something different. I only knew one method to earn an income and that was to work for someone else. There was no training for this scenario in life, I was not recession-proof. I did not have the awareness of diversification, i.e. creating multiple streams of incomes, so you don't put all your eggs into one basket.

Now we had relocated, we had a roof over our heads and food on the table, which was the most important thing. Not forgetting Jen was about six months pregnant at this point. The next step for me was signing on at the jobcentre to claim the benefits that I was entitled to. For me, this was the most soul-destroying thing I have ever done. I never ever thought I'd be in that situation. I had a Master's degree when I lost my job and had thought I was invincible.

"I'm not supposed to be claiming benefits and living off the government when I have this Masters qualification. I have what it takes to be in full-time employment."

This is what I was saying to myself. It just didn't make any sense. I now had a full-time job, which was to look for a secure and stable income. I did not want us to be claiming benefits for the rest of our life.

"What would Jen think of me? What would my family and her family think of me?"

I was determined to find something that I was a good fit for, and also a role that I knew I would enjoy, but most importantly, a role that would match my skill set and experience from my previous job. So in other words, this was quite specialised. Testing transmission systems is not your typical job that you can get in any high street. It is a unique skill set to certain industries and geographical locations.

Time was ticking and the baby's arrival was imminent. But then I had the breakthrough that I needed. I received an email on the 30th July from a recruitment specialist.

"Further to your recent application for the position of Test Engineer I am pleased to advise you that our client has expressed an interest in interviewing you for this

role. I would like to speak to you as soon as possible, so that we can arrange a suitable date and time for the interview."

This fantastic opportunity was regarding a new position for a Transmission Test Engineer in the aerospace industry. I could not believe it. I was super excited about the chance to test helicopter gearboxes. The job was in Yeovil, Somerset, which meant a relocation from South London. Despite this, I grabbed the opportunity with both hands and did not hesitate. Of course, I ran it by my partner first.

The recruitment agency went off and did their magic and got me a face-to-face interview.

"Fran, I write further to our telephone conversation today regarding the interview that has been arranged for you with AgustaWestland.
I confirm the details are as follows:- Tuesday 11th August 2009 at 11:00."

Maybe this rejection four months ago wasn't so bad after all. New opportunity...New baby on the way...New start.

I got suited up and made myself look somewhat decent for the interview. I was not experienced with interviews, so I was very nervous. But I did not know any other way of being, other than to just be myself.

I knew the interview went really well, when I spoke about my experience with six speed automatic transmissions, with integrated electronic brake and clutch systems, torque converters and complex test rig control systems. The following day, I received this email:

"Fran, as discussed, following my conversation with AgustaWestland today, I would like to confirm that they would like to make you the offer of Transmission Test Engineer to work onsite at Yeovil. The offer is an initial six-month

contract. However, as discussed there should be plenty more work down there after the initial period."

I could not believe it. I wasn't too surprised to be honest, but it was such a great feeling. It was a feeling of gratitude for someone to give me an opportunity to show my capabilities. I felt appreciated again. I had the feeling of self-worth, a sense of pride, a sense of hope. I have always believed in myself and it was the expectation of other people believing in me.

I told Jen and my family the great news straight away. They were all very proud of me, but I didn't have much time to celebrate. My start date in the new role was the second of September, 2009. Logistically this was a challenge, as Jen was heavily pregnant. We were staying in London and my new job was at least a two-hour drive away. So, we decided that Jen would stay with her family, and I would move down to Poole on my own in the interim. The reason we agreed to move to Poole instead of Yeovil was because one of Jen's good friends lived in Poole and there was a spare bedroom that I could use. So, the plan was for me to start my new job and once Jen got close to giving birth, I would drive back up to London to be there for her. When our baby girl was born, Jen would eventually move down. And that's exactly what we did.

It was nine months from the time I was served my four weeks' notice to move into a rental property in Canford Heath, Poole, with my new young family. It was a great feeling to have a bit more stability in our lives, but it all comes back to what caused this change in our lives…A company rejecting me, a company not believing in me.

"They weren't better than me. What's so special about them?"
"Why didn't they lose their jobs?"
"Why me?"

All of this changed because of the human resources department not knowing my true worth, my true value in life. However, living with a partner I loved and our newborn baby girl, everything else became irrelevant. Nothing else mattered.

The negative force of the Jedi

My biggest passion is motorsport, and this was the time when I was volunteering in a couple of motorsport teams. One of those was a championship known as Formula Jedi. I actually came across this team when I was studying my Masters degree in motorsport vehicle dynamics. The owner of one of the cars allowed students to gain hands-on experience working on real racing cars. This included setting up the suspension geometry (camber, toe, ride height, castor, etc.) After completing my Masters, I was so passionate to continue working with this team. Fortunately, I was given permission to support every race weekend and help the team in any way I could. In other words, I was a mechanic for the driver. My duties included checking the condition of the car, refuelling, repairing any damages, managing the data acquisition system, ensuring the video cameras are recording, and keeping it clean. This was for every session.

I was super excited, as this was, and still is, a huge passion of mine. I travelled with the team all over the UK and even around Europe. We used to do a road trip to the Spa Francorchamps F1 racetrack in Belgium. This is one of my favourite tracks in the world. I was in my element living this lifestyle and I really enjoyed being part of a team that I thought appreciated me. However, all of a sudden this changed, and I was no longer needed anymore.

The dynamics of the team began to change when new team members came into the team. The team took on two young female mechanics, who were also passionate about motorsport. I was still doing the same job, but I started to notice how the girls were getting far more attention and that I was slowly being pushed out. This wasn't jealousy, it was just a fact. I was excluded from social events, such as going out for drinks. The turning point was when I did not get invited to a large formal black-tie event for all of the championship teams. The only way I found out about it was through Facebook. I saw photos of them all out having a great time without me.

This really was the turning point for me, and I came to the realisation that I was no longer wanted in this team. It was heartbreaking to realise I was not considered a vital asset within the team. I was so upset and I felt completely betrayed and abandoned. I was very angry, and yet confused as to what was going on. I didn't understand why I was no longer wanted or needed in this team. The team that I helped for many years. To me, I worked very hard, and I was always fully committed to helping this team be a championship-winning team. It made no sense to me.

"How could all of my efforts be taken away from me so quickly? What had I done wrong? Wasn't my commitment enough?" ...

As much as I tried to look on the bright side and understand that everything happens for a reason, it still didn't make up for the feelings of being rejected by the people who were once so important to me. It felt as if all of my hard work meant nothing in the end; like it was all wasted effort on my part.

I had always believed that dedication and hard work would pay off eventually; however, this experience showed me that wasn't necessarily true. People don't always take into account how much effort you put into something or even acknowledge it when you do succeed - sometimes they prefer to take advantage instead. That realisation was devastating, but also gave me insight into what kind of person I wanted to be: someone who respects others, appreciates them for what they do, recognises their efforts, and is simply grateful for any success achieved through collaboration.

It had been a long and difficult journey that ultimately led me to the realisation that I was no longer needed in the team. All of my hard work, dedication, and commitment to the group had not been enough to convince them that I was capable of meeting their expectations. Despite my best efforts, I had failed to impress, and as a result, I was deemed surplus to requirements.

This experience had certainly taught me an important lesson: sometimes we may not be up for certain tasks, or roles even though we believe in ourselves. The dynamics of the team may just not work; however, understanding our limitations is essential if we are ever going to make meaningful improvements in life, be it personally or professionally. I came to the conclusion that it was time to accept this rejection and move on with my life. Yet another one of life's lessons.

CHAPTER FIVE

BATTLING WITH THE ENEMY

Why did he do this?... Only he knows.

It was June 2014, when I decided to leave the aerospace industry and return to the automotive industry, which felt more aligned with my passion for cars. So I went back to the very same job, the same one I started out as a transmission rig test engineer in 2009, the job where I had been working with my best friend. I was thinking of all those great memories we had and how great it would be to create many new ones. However, this time it was completely different. So much had changed, including my perception of people and subsequently, I found this phase of my life painful and traumatic.

Unfortunately, my friend no longer had the same level of care and support he had shown five years earlier. He was different and he seemed a lot more controlling and full of power. I simply did not recognise him anymore. I had flashbacks of when we used to go fishing together, when we would go for pints, watch matches together at the football stadium, or meeting his family for lunch.

It got so bad that he started bullying me, not physically, but emotionally. The department was now operating what they called a

'Tea School', and they would rotate who was responsible for keeping the tea school up to date. This was making sure there was enough tea, coffee, milk, and sugar in the kitchen for us all to enjoy. When it was my turn, I got what was needed at the time. I don't remember the exact details, but I was eventually accused of theft. In other words, they thought I was taking the tea school money and not buying what we needed in the kitchen.

That was not the only issue in the department. Because there were a number of test rigs to manage, I was given one where I had to commission a very complex transmission durability sign-off test. I was working long days, 6am to 6pm, and was always the first in the office and the last to leave. Of course, I was recording the hours that I worked in my weekly timesheets, as I always did. However, I did not think this would create the problem that it did. Each week, after submitting my timesheet, my so-called friend would send me an email, warning me not to submit so many hours. All I was doing was working extremely hard to get the test completed, so we could tell the transmission supplier that the test was running. However, the situation soon escalated out of control.

This carried on for a number of weeks and it got to a point where my former friend asked me to come outside as he wanted to talk to me. We were standing outside the test rig building on the edge of the footpath, by the grass and it was in this moment when I saw a completely different side to him. I could see the anger and rage in his eyes and read his body language. He verbally abused me and had no hesitation in telling me what he really thought of me. I was shocked, speechless, and without a doubt, extremely hurt and upset. He said to me not in so many words that he was going to make sure that I paid for this. I could see what was to come. For a minute, I thought it was going to get physical. Gloves off, literally. I was preparing myself to go into battle with the enemy on the grass on site, in the middle of the day. The worst part of it however was that I knew our friendship was now over.

Although the conversation was over in only a few minutes, it felt like hours. I felt like a naughty schoolboy, who had just been told off by the headteacher. It really was a horrible experience. I was thirty-two at the time, not six, and I was treated as if I had hit another boy in the playground. When in fact, I was applying the knowledge that I learned, and I was doing my very best to get the complex automatic transmission durability test up and running for our supplier.

I was reported to our line manager, which I knew I would be. It was a couple of days later when this time my line manager dragged me outside (not literally!). My former friend had arranged for this to happen, but I was not expecting what was to come. I'll never forget walking over to the building next door, going upstairs, and into the meeting room. This conversation was just not what I was planning to have that day. The line manager was also very blunt with me. Like the conversation with my former friend, it was only a short discussion, but it felt like an eternity. It felt like being in the school headmaster's office once again and that I was going to be punished. I genuinely thought it would just be a verbal warning, even though I had done absolutely nothing wrong. I was told I was letting the team down, I was not listening to anyone or following the guidelines. But he didn't recognise, realise I was the first person in the morning and the last one to leave in the evening, trying to get the test commissioned on my own, with very little support. I was working more hours than I should have and there was no recognition, gratitude, or acknowledgment. That's what hurt me the most. My hard work, effort, and commitment were not appreciated or acknowledged.

My line manager finally came out with what he really wanted to say to me. He was not afraid to throw the big punches (with words). He said that he didn't see me fitting into this team and that he was going to terminate my contract, with immediate effect. I was to leave the role as a transmission test engineer (for the second time).

My heart was broken, I could not believe it…another four weeks' notice was served to me. My world was collapsing, and I truly wanted to give up on everything. This, however, was the moment when the penny finally dropped. I was coming to terms with reality, and how toxic the corporate world really was. This was a big wake-up call for me in experiencing firsthand what it's like to be treated with so much disrespect, with no gratitude, in an environment and company that was renowned for looking after its most important assets… it's people…it's staff. What a load of nonsense.

"Was this really the corporate world? This can't be it."

Those were the longest four weeks of my life. The damage was done, and I no longer wanted to work with these guys anymore. This could not be repaired…accused of theft, brought outside and verbally abused, and then being told I wasn't in the team anymore… It was game over.

The first thing I did after that last conversation was to message Jen and my family, and tell them, again, that I had just lost another job. This was another moment of me failing at what I was doing. I felt so hollow… empty inside like I was not cut out for this corporate game.

It was very uncomfortable for me in that environment, knowing I was no longer wanted in the team. I was no longer trusted, respected, or appreciated. I did everything I could to get out of the office when I was at work. I found it unbearable. The first place I went after that uncomfortable conversation was, I walked back into the transmission test rig facility, walked in the door downstairs, and told my friends, the fitters, what had just happened. They were shocked and could not believe it. They were so supportive and were by my side the whole time. As I said, those were the longest four weeks of my life and I did everything I did to avoid being in that building. I would go for walks around the engineering site, I would sit over in the canteen for an hour at a time, with a hot chocolate, just to get away. It truly was a horrible feeling and experience. It was like I was imprisoned and was not allowed out.

"How do I overcome this?"

Engagement to abandonment

At this point, I had two young children, Faye (5 years old) and Sara (3 years old) to provide for and to protect. I was now starting to lose trust and belief in what I was doing. I was beginning to have self-doubt and lose all confidence in being able to do anything in life. The last thing I wanted was for Faye and Sara to be disappointed in me. I know they were still very young, but I didn't want them growing up and thinking I was a failure or a father who could not provide for his family.

This had huge implications for me personally…I was in such a dark place, and it was affecting my family as well. I was living away from home at the time, in rented accommodation, Monday to Friday and sadly, I never got to see my children. My relationship was deteriorating, and it felt like my world was collapsing right in front of my eyes. I sacrificed my life, and my family for this company, this brand that I looked up to so much.

I felt so disconnected from my loved ones, disconnected from reality. Any time I was home with my family, we would argue. It got to a point where Faye, who was only five years old at the time, would say things like, "I wish daddy was dead". Hearing this broke my heart. It felt like I had failed already as a father. I suffered from depression and was starting to take anti-depressants. I had no motivation anymore to do anything, and everything in my life was disappearing or was evaporating into thin air. I was losing hope in life. I now struggled to see success…it was no longer in front of me. The pain was unbearable. The basic joys of having a happy family were non-existent for me. The days were becoming darker and darker without any hope for change. I felt completely trapped and was suffocating from the lack of control in my life.

"What's the point in carrying on? I have no reason to be here. I have failed."

"I'm fighting a losing battle."

While all this was going on, I was in the process of saving my relationship with my daughter's mother. You see, we had been together since April 2008, and things happened very quickly. Within a year we were living together and expecting our first child, Faye. We eventually even bought a house together. We got the keys the week before Sara was born in 2009. Everything was going well, I guess we were in a typical relationship, nothing out of the ordinary. I knew that I wanted to have a normal happy family and I never wanted to lose Jen, and even though we had many tough moments, I always thought we would get through it.

I plucked up the courage to go out and buy Jen an engagement ring. I wanted to marry her and for us to be a happy loving family. The proposal was nothing too extreme, I got down on one knee and asked her to marry me in our living room at home. For me, it felt so surreal being engaged and we had so much to plan for the wedding. Wasting no time, we booked the venue, the photographer, and were making great progress with the wedding plans. I must admit, I was scared…the thought of being married did terrify me.

However, this all escalated out of control and got out of hand very quickly. I took Jen to Spain in October 2015, where we met my family. My brother was working in an Irish bar in Costa Del Sol at the time, so I thought it would be nice to all spend time together out there with my new fiancé. However, one night out on the balcony, my relationship was about to come to an end.

My family, including Jen, were all having a few drinks and the conversation was flowing. We were having a great time. However, the atmosphere changed when Jen opened up about me and our relationship. She said that she was happy for me to go out and get a job to earn the money, while she stayed at home looking after the children, with no intention of ever finding a job. She made it sounds like she didn't take the relationship seriously and that she was using me to get what she wanted. It was like she was joking, but in fact, she was very serious. All of my family suddenly saw red flags and alarm bells started ringing. What they were hearing was such a big wake-up call for them. Me being me, I didn't quite see it the way they saw it and when Jen went to bed, my family were not afraid to share their opinion with me.

This was the moment the penny dropped. I didn't realise the unhealthy relationship that I was in. A relationship that I had been in for over seven years. That night I walked into the bathroom and broke down with emotion. It finally hit me that I was in a relationship that wasn't working. I was engaged to Jen at the time, and I thought, how can I continue to live a lie? I could not go into a marriage feeling this way. So, I waited until we returned home to the UK before I confronted Jen about my feelings. This was when things changed. We were never the same again. The wedding was called off and my dreams were shattered.

Family life was so difficult, and it was unfair to have our children caught up in the middle of all this. In April 2016, I started the process for us to consider family mediation.

This was eventually arranged for us in Dorchester and we both agreed to attend. However, after the second session, Jen refused to continue with the program and admitted she no longer wanted to be with me anymore. My heart sank. I was literally heartbroken, and there was nothing more I could do to save us. That was it. It was around May 2016, when it had to go through solicitors. It had turned so sour that we had no other choice.

In October 2016, the day of Faye's seventh birthday, everything appeared to be going well. We all had a lovely day on Faye's big day. It was around bath time and winding down for bed when things took a turn for the worst. A domestic unexpectedly kicked off between Jen and I, while our girls were having their bath. It was nothing out of the ordinary, just a heated discussion. Unfortunately, it was in front of the kids, which is not the way it should be. I don't have many regrets, but arguing in front of my children is one of them. However, I did not abuse anyone in my family, and I never would, but for some reason, Jen threatened to call the police on me. I think this was her way of having power, and authority over me. To be honest, I didn't think anything of it. However, about twenty minutes later, I heard a knock on the front door. I thought to myself, "She hasn't, has she?" I was upstairs in our ensuite toilet and to my amazement, I saw two policemen in their high-viz uniforms standing there in my bedroom. They wanted to question me there and then in my bedroom. I was shocked and speechless. I had to sit on the bed, I simply couldn't believe what Jen had done.

This was the night that changed my life forever. It was decided that Jen would take our girls to their grandparents' house. I knew this was the last time that I would ever live with my daughters. I'll never forget that moment seeing my children being taken away from me with a police escort. I felt so many emotions; hurt, anger, shock, confusion, betrayal and rejection. The house felt like the loneliest place, when I was sitting there on my own reflecting on what had just happened. One minute I'm with my family bathing our children and the next, I'm being questioned by police in my bedroom, while my partner and children are escorted out of the house by the police. I realised I had one major decision to make and that was what I was going to do with my life. One option was to buy as much alcohol as possible and drink myself into the ground, the other was to pick myself up from what had just happened and prove to myself and everyone that I was a decent human, capable of so many things. Although option one was tempting, I chose the latter.

CHAPTER SIX

YOU'VE GOT TO BE KIDDING ME

Is it time to surrender?

Returning to my career and following my experience in the transmission test rig facility, I managed to be creative and find a new role within the same company. However, this time, it was in a different department. Now my goal was to move on from what had happened, not let it get to me, and most importantly prove to myself that I had what it takes to be part of this company.

So I sent my CV to the head of the Chassis Engineering department, for him to pass it down to his entire team. I had many years of experience as a rig test engineer, but I now wanted to have exposure to vehicle testing. I wanted to develop prototype vehicles on public roads and on test tracks, which is why I reached out to the Chassis team.

It did not take long for an opportunity to present itself. One of the line managers was keen to enrol me into his team, where I would measure objective ride comfort on all vehicle products, including benchmarking competitor vehicles. This was an incredible experience for me, as I had not done anything like this before.

I was in this role for two and a half years, and in that time, there were a few manager changes. That did not affect me in any way. I was still doing the same testing and working very hard. However, it was the last manager I had that changed the dynamic of my relationship with the team. I could tell that our personalities were going to clash. I found him extremely controlling. Not in a typical manager way, instead, it was as though his ego was thriving on having authority.

Unfortunately, one day things completely changed. We had a one-to-one meeting arranged one morning. I was already nervous and intimidated going into the meeting. However, I held my nerve and held my head high, as I was about to prove my true worth to the company. At the time of our discussion, there was a request in the department for volunteer engineers to support sign-off testing out in Spain. I spoke with the manager requesting additional support, and he was more than happy for me to join the team out in Spain. But when I brought this to my meeting, it was somewhat dismissed. For some unknown reason, my manager was adamant that I was not to go, and refused to sign off this opportunity for me to work in Spain. It was like he had a serious problem with me and although I confronted him and we discussed the matter, I distinctly remember him saying, *"I expect better from you, Fran".*

Not only was I shocked, but I was angry and upset. *"What more did he want me to do?"* I was fulfilling all of the tasks I was asked to do, was completing the objective ride measurements, and now I was submitting a request to support urgent sign-off testing. I was going above and beyond my duties. *"Why did he say that to me?"*

This was another form of rejection…I did not know what was going on. I could not process this in my head. I was so angry with him, that I very nearly leaned over the desk and assaulted him. I was that angry. But it was at this moment, I knew that I could no longer work for this person. I did not like his attitude towards me, the team, or the company. I simply lost all confidence and trust in working for someone who did not respect or value me as a highly capable test engineer.

Am I just a number to you?

I immediately decided to search for a different role, one in which I was aligned with the team vision, where I would get the respect that I deserved. I also wanted to work in an area where technology dominated the industry. That was why I connected with the ADAS (Assisted Driving and Autonomous Systems) department. This is the team that develops features such as lane keep assist, adaptive cruise control (ACC) and blind spot monitoring. This department really caught my attention at the time, and I was so excited to get my foot in the door with a great opportunity. In January 2018, I was given the responsibility of being a lead ACC development engineer, where I would validate the performance of this adaptive cruise control system on all of the company's new model variants. Things were great. Everything I recently experienced was all in the past and I was starting out on a new adventure building up new skills.

However, things began to change again for me. When I was given an exciting project of managing the training program for advanced level-5 that we were rolling out around the company, I discovered how my voice was not heard. It was as if my opinion didn't matter. After so much time and effort working on this, the project was taken from me.

In my experience, the engineering world is an incredibly difficult one to navigate, when faced with job losses and contract terminations. I had no understanding of how to navigate the system, nor any sense of feeling valued or worthy in such a cold and unforgiving environment. I felt as though I was stuck in a cycle of manipulation and control, where I had zero say in my own development. The idea of being treated as a number seemed like an ever-looming reality. I found myself feeling increasingly helpless, unable to find any hope from this bleak situation.

It was then that I decided to make a change. To break the cycle of helplessness and hopelessness, I chose to invest in my personal growth, transformation, and learning new skills - digital skills in particular - so that I could help others who were also facing rejection at every turn.

I began by seeking mentors who could guide me through this challenging process of healing and self-discovery. With their help, I learned the importance of resilience; how to maintain perspective during difficult times; how to remain focused on long-term goals; and ultimately learning how adaptability can be used as a tool for achieving success despite having been fired or laid off due to economic hardship.

Through this journey, I also became acutely aware that there is strength and power found within each individual's unique skill set; something which we all take for granted too often. This newfound awareness allowed me to use my acquired skills for more than just finding a job — it enabled me to pursue more meaningful work that would not only be satisfying, but also another way to generate an income from helping others, instead of feeling like just a number in the corporate engineering world. This was my epiphany moment. Even though I continued to lose more employment contracts, I now have belief and hope that there is more than one way (the old broken traditional way) to earn a living. I mastered the skill of being open-minded to new opportunities and possibilities.

I have a voice…please listen.

In the middle of all this, I found myself tangled up in another scenario, where this time the rejection came from a financial provider. It was 27th May 2016, the weekend of my friend's stag party weekend. I was in the middle of sorting out finance for a second-hand car that I was purchasing. Although I didn't normally do this kind of thing, I bought a 2008 Ford Mondeo from a backstreet garage in Bournemouth, UK.

However, instead of weekend cruising, it was one problem after another with the car. I eventually got to a point where I had enough. I told the car dealer that I was handing it back to them, as it was not fit for purpose. Somehow this escalated and spiralled out of control. The owner of the car dealership did not listen to me, or acknowledge what I was saying. This car was a death trap and it nearly killed me a few times. It wasn't until I moved house, when I was eventually taken to court over this for not paying the balance of the finance. It was around June 2018, and I had a strong case. This whole situation was so upsetting and distressing. To me, this was yet another rejection that I had to face head-on. I built myself a case, as I was fighting for my rights. Being an engineer, I wrote a thorough case report that detailed all of the anomalies on the vehicle. Here is how I concluded my witness statement…

"To summarise, this vehicle had the following faults:
Multiple tyre puncture (on new and used tyres) due to cracked alloy wheels.
Many electrical fault codes.
Engine de-rating.
Significant steering vibration.
Significant vibration under braking.
Poor DAB and radio performance.
Poor air conditioning.

My conclusion is that the vehicle suspension was modified with aftermarket parts, which made the chassis to have a stiffness that exceeded the limit of the wheel. This was not related to my driving style. I believe that the garage did not fully inspect the condition of the vehicle and performed the MOT on this vehicle in an unacceptable manner. I believe that the facts stated in this statement are true to the best of my knowledge. I am currently in a new separate Finance Agreement with the same financial company, for a significantly larger monthly payment and a vehicle that I thoroughly enjoy and feel safe to bring my children in. I request for the Court to set the judgement aside, to enable myself and my family to move on with our lives without this stress. I also request for the Default Notice to be removed from my credit file with immediate effect..."

Can you see why I was dejected, and again, experienced the pain of not having a voice, not being listened to and not being respected? This experience of rejection was different from all of my other situations. This time it was with a financial company that felt they had insatiable power and authority over me. But because of my persistence and my attention to detail in my report, I won the court case. It was a hollow, but triumphant victory and throughout the process, I stuck to my principles and never gave up.

My story is not just about overcoming setbacks; it is about discovering inner strengths through the hard times, recognising my worth, even when rejected by employers, loving partners, and finance companies. Most importantly, it's about believing in myself, no matter what hand life deals me.

Coming back to my engineering career...The one that wasn't going so well in the ADAS department. Well, here's the thing. I got a familiar email on the 31st of January, 2019...

"Morning Fran, I am sorry to say that notice has been served on your contract with JLR, making your last working day 28/02/19."

How do you think I felt? Job loss number three…(from the same company)

I felt let down by the company.

I felt let down by the corporate world.

I felt like just a number…not a human being.

I felt angry.

I felt humiliated.

I felt unworthy.

I felt determined to pursue new digital skills.

I felt my life was an illusion.

What is it about me?

Again, I found myself in familiar territory searching for a new corporate 9-to-5 job. By now I was getting so used to updating my CV, contacting the same agencies, and claiming benefits, it felt like groundhog day. It had to be the most depressing thing that I did and it was far from living my best life and vision.

The next job did not come until June 2019, so four months after my previous role. At this point, I had zero motivation and passion to continue with engineering, or in fact, any job in the corporate world, where I would be working for someone, getting bossed around, manipulated and bullied. The fear of rejection was so strong. It was off the scale, and this fear was taking over my life. It was eating me up inside. I did not want, or need this, particularly as I had a family to provide for and a life to live.

I must admit, the job was great. In fact, it probably was the best job I ever had, in terms of the high performance, and the sheer scale of the project I was working on. This role was contracting (again!), through an agency, and my job title was a Transmission Calibration Engineer, for a company based out in Austria, so it was a very unique setup. I was based in the UK. This was for a very special project that was a collaboration between Mercedes AMG HPP (High Performance Powertrain) and Multimatic (the project owner).

I was working on a very unique hypercar project called "Project One", and I was the only UK representative to manage the transmission calibration and software on Project One. This was the first time ever that Mercedes AMG attempted to put their Formula one hybrid powertrain system into a production road car that would drive on public roads. This was the first time this was ever attempted. Yes, it was the same championship winning powertrain system that powered Lewis Hamilton's Formula one racing car. I couldn't believe it. The team wanted me, Fran Wilson, to support this project. They trusted me, they believed in me and my capability. This did not feel anything close to rejection. If anything, it was acceptance... acceptance that I was good enough to contribute to this team of extraordinary engineers. I felt so much pride. I finally thought to myself, maybe, just maybe this was my chance where I was recognised and rewarded for all my efforts up until now. Even though, at the back of my mind, my dream was now something completely different (building a business helping other people overcome rejection), and I wanted to gain this once-in-a-lifetime opportunity. How could I turn down this insane job? The engineer is always there inside of me, and there he was, very excited, ready to support achieving the impossible with Mercedes AMG and everyone involved.

I was in this role when the devastating global Covid pandemic hit us all. Everything was going so well in the job, and we all adapted professionally to the health risks. What made it possible to continue working was the technology in the world we live in today, I was able to work remotely from home. Yes, I was able to commission a brand new gearbox from the comfort of my own home. This meant I could communicate with a gearbox that was either still in the vehicle build workshop, or at a test track about to go out and do some high-speed testing. As long as I could communicate with the laptop in the car, which was connected and actively communicating with the gearbox, I could simply use "Remote Desktop Connection" to do what I needed to do.

I know…this is crazy. I was pinching myself, saying, "Am I really controlling this two-million-pound hypercar gearbox and changing gears, opening and closing the clutch from my home?" Sometimes just in my underwear! Like I said, I felt so proud of myself for having the skill set to be able to do this.

Some of the highlights of this role was when I was at the test tracks with some of the development vehicles. Unfortunately, I never got to drive the cars (due to policies around agency contractors), but I would be a passenger, with a laptop, doing transmission updates and data collection, around the test track. I also attended a private and exclusive event at the famous Brands Hatch racing track in Kent, UK, where I was responsible for updating two or three development vehicles with the latest transmission software and calibrations. This event was working with a professional racing driver, who provided subjective feedback to me on the performance of the gearshifts.

As you can tell, being super passionate about motorsport, I was in a job that ticked all of my boxes. I was really enjoying it. Even though like any other job, this did have many political challenges, which I faced on a daily basis. However, this was a job that got me a step closer to my ultimate engineering career goal-working as an engineer in Formula one, the pinnacle of motorsport. That was the reason I pursued my engineering career in the UK all those years ago back in 2003. Well, my engineering career technically began in the year 2000, so in actual fact, I spent over 20 years building this dream. However, this dream was about to be shattered yet again.

I'll never forget the day. I was in the brand-new production facility, where they were building some of these development vehicles, where they were going to build all 275 production vehicles. It was a very impressive facility, and I was becoming familiar with the setup there. I was in the process of updating the latest development builds when I got a phone call from my manager, who was based in Austria. I thought it was just a routine call, where he was just checking in with me to see how things were going. But then I could tell that this was not one of those calls.

It was a very brief call and he got straight to the point. He said the business was having to adapt due to the pandemic, and the business plan now was to remove all UK support (me), as they wanted to focus all of their resources on European projects. So, in other words, my role was being removed, and I was surplus to requirements. My heart sank. Even though this was now the fourth or fifth time it had happened to me, the pain always felt the same. It did not get any easier. Again, I felt unworthy, just a number, disrespected, unwanted, disappointed, and angry.

Unless you experience this relentless sequence of job losses, you will never know the feeling of having an unstable and insecure career path. Although maybe you can relate to this. Do you resonate with this career rejection? Does your family know what it's like to lose so many jobs and the stress, and the anxiety it causes?

This is why I was still passionate about continuing to work on other opportunities and projects. This was always happening in the background. In fact, these rejections were my fuel to keep pushing forward. They were my "Why". The reason I was doing what I was doing. Somehow, I found the strength, resilience, and relentlessness to keep going, pick myself up again, and again, and again, dust myself down, and move forward.

I no longer felt aligned with my vision

It was another six months before I found my next job. As you may remember, employment opportunities during the Covid pandemic were rare. Purchase orders could not get signed off, which was the issue I had in my next role. Even though I secured a permanent role in April 2021, my only permanent role in my career believe it or not, the projects were not getting signed off, so I was not given any work to do. It was like the universe was trying to tell me that I was not meant for this corporate world. I was sitting at home for four months, waiting for engineering work on the project we agreed on. Fortunately, I was not told to leave like every other job, but I still felt the company let me down, as they had broken their promise to me. So, this time, I decided to leave on my own terms.

It wasn't long before I got my next job, and the reason for this was not because of what I knew, it was because of who I knew. As I loved the "Project One" job so much, I reached out to a contact in Mercedes AMG, whom I worked with previously, asking him if there was an opportunity to join his team. A short time later, I was having an MS Teams interview with the performance engineering team manager. Immediately after the call, when I was having a look around the shops, I got an email offering me a job at Mercedes AMG HPP. I couldn't believe it. I was now one step closer to my dream of becoming the engineer I'd always wanted to be. In fact, the manager that hired me had actually interviewed me about four years earlier, and unfortunately turned me down. He did not want me in his team then, but he did now. I was super excited.

However, I was still not aligned with working for someone else, and I always had that in the back of my mind. I guess this showed when I was on the job. For some reason, I could not get going. I did not have the drive, the motivation, or the passion for this role that I thought I would. Certainly, the Fran Wilson of four years ago would have bitten your arm off to have this job. But why was I not feeling it? Maybe it was simply the fear of rejection. The fear of being let down again. Remembering back on all those times when teams didn't want me. Was this fear of rejection haunting me? Or was it the thought of being bossed around and controlled by someone else? Looking back, I think it was a combination of the two.

It didn't take long for my manager to recognise that I was not performing as he expected and in one of our rare meetings, he did actually say to me, *"Fran, you're underperforming."*

Hearing this lowered my confidence even more, and it simply got to a point, where he sat me down again to have another discussion. I knew exactly where the conversation was going, and he told me it was to do with a business resource issue, but he basically told me that my contract was being terminated early. Like I said previously, this type of conversation never gets easier.

Let's talk men and mental health

Men and mental health typically comes with social stigma. Fortunately, we are easing into a better space with this topic, however so much is still lagging behind. According to the National Institute of Mental Health, one in five people live with mental illness in the United States.

Similarly in the UK, I found that mental health statistics show that over a third of men (35%) think they've had a diagnosable mental health condition at some point in their life. To get a better understanding of how men think and interact with their mental health, a survey was commissioned of 1,000 men in the UK.

77% of men polled said they have suffered from common mental health symptoms like anxiety, stress or depression.

40% of men have never spoken to anyone about their mental health.

29% of those who haven't done so say they are "too embarrassed" to speak about it, while 20% say there is a "negative stigma" on the issue.

The biggest cause of mental health issues in men's lives are work (32%), their finances (31%) and their health (23%).

40% of men polled said they would take thoughts of suicide or self-harm to compel them to seek professional help.

I found this statistic in particular quite alarming and concerning. Statistically, men tend to fall into dangerous, self-destructive behaviours, rather than seek professional help for their mental health. They may avoid or delay seeking treatment because of concerns about being treated differently, or due to perceptions that having a mental health issue diminishes their masculinity, saying they are "too embarrassed" or there is a "negative stigma" attached to the issue.

Unfortunately, this is exactly how I felt. I thought, no I don't need professional help, I don't need therapy. I can find my own unique solution. For me, stubbornness was definitely driving my decisions. I could not face reality and concede to my mental health issues. I guess, men don't want to look weak, but at the end of the day, we are human as well, and we do suffer. As a society, we must be open and reach for help. No matter who we are.

When being the "good guy" backfires!

I know firsthand what it's like to be the good guy in a relationship; to have a partner who is so controlling and manipulating that it simply destroys your identity. But there is only so much as men can take as well. We do have a limit, just like women. There is a threshold to what we can withstand. I always come back to my engineering analogies, and say that when men are pushed to our limits, we start fatiguing in a certain area and after a certain time, we reach our limit, and we break.

Our mind, our emotions, our thoughts can no longer take it anymore. However, we don't want our failure to be seen by anyone, which is why men are reluctant to be open and honest about it and seek professional help. I guess this also comes from a lack of understanding from a male perspective around a sense of fear. However, I know that it's okay to talk and we must eradicate the notion that men don't suffer from mental health issues… we do.

CHAPTER SEVEN

MY LIFE... ON HER TERMS!

We first spoke on my brother's wedding day

Now it's time for the one that hurt me the most...My life on her terms. This is the best way of describing what happened in this particular relationship that I was in. This was without doubt the toughest chapter for me to write. I know I have so many other family rejection moments that included my children, but for some reason this is the one that hurt the most. Maybe it's because it was over such a long period with constant abuse. However, it's something that I must do, so that I can prove to myself and to you reading this, that I do have the power to overcome any form of rejection and abandonment that comes my way.

Before I go on, I want to be clear that until this very day, I have nothing against this person. In fact, I have always loved her... I did my absolute best for her, always believed in her potential...and I always will...I simply have to share my experience. This is my humble and honest opinion, which I'm entitled to...without judgement. This is a long path of rejection and destruction that I get to share. As I said, this is something I must do, and get to do. I know I'm not the only person who has experienced this type of pain and suffering. There are many of you reading this who can resonate with the life-changing and traumatic experience I'm about to share with you.

It was Monday, the 31st of July 2017 in Dublin…my brother's wedding day. I sat there in the morning with my cup of tea, very excited that my brother was getting married to an amazing long-term partner. They had met in an Irish bar in Spain, and they were meant to be together. They were so aligned with one another and were certainly on the same frequency, which is the way it should be.

Before I had a shower and got dressed, I decided to send another few messages to some women on the dating app, Plenty of Fish. I knew at this point, my chances of having a conversation with someone were extremely low. I find that no one wants to talk on dating apps…ironic eh!

But then one message came through and it was from a lovely, gorgeous, sweet female. I shall change her name to protect her identity. So, let's call her Lauren. We didn't talk much that day, but she seemed so lovely and caring. I was very excited that someone finally seemed to appreciate me and wanted to connect. It wasn't really until after the wedding that we really started chatting with each other.

We arranged to go on our first date on the 8th of August, 2017, when I was back in the UK. suggested a lovely country pub, near where she lived. It's a beautiful little pub and was the perfect place to meet. I don't know what made me do it, but I thought being the nice, charming, and generous guy I am, it would be a nice gesture to get Lauren a gift. So I went to my local supermarket and chose a selection of items; a small artificial plant, a box of chocolates, a can of her favourite alcoholic drink.

I'll never forget driving to the pub, waiting in my car. We met in the car park and I gave her the bag of gifts. She was so happy and surprised to receive these on our first date. That earned me a few brownie points, I think! We went inside and had a couple of drinks. I don't know what it was but, I felt so relaxed around Lauren and I found it so easy to have a simple, relaxed conversation with her. I could have stayed chatting with her all night. When we were leaving, we had a small kiss on the lips. It was perfect and I drove home so happy.

At the start of our relationship, it was infatuation and an obsession, waiting for each other's text messages. It was such a nice feeling. Our next date was a big one…an interesting one with a twist…We went to an Indian restaurant, which was literally at the end of the road where Lauren lived. We had an amazing time again. The conversation was flowing, and I didn't want it to end. One thing I'll never ever forget was when Lauren asked if I would help her to do a food shop in the supermarket, which was literally next door to the restaurant. I didn't think anything of it. In fact, I was happy I could spend more time with her. It was lovely.

Walking around the store it seemed like we had known each other for a long time. We filled up the shopping trolley with food she needed for herself and her son, who has a rare learning disability, known as Williams Syndrome. I even decided to pay for it when we got to the cashier. Another few extra points for me! We then loaded up the boot of her car with the shopping. Then the moment came. We had our first proper kiss. It felt so nice and I felt like I was in heaven. I truly thought I had found "the one".

I don't know why I did what I did next, but I simply had to do it. I booked us a lovely holiday for four nights in Manhattan, New York. It was planned for mid-December, 2017. I did this just four months after meeting her. Lauren could not believe I did it. She was so happy, and that's all I wanted. In the meantime, and after only two months of meeting each other, Lauren decided it would be great to have her engagement finger measured. I'll never forget it, she was a size M. It felt like the universe was telling me that Lauren and I were meant for each other. We were meant to get married and grow old together. I was so excited about that idea. I was starting to plan it out in my head. A few months later, I took her away to Dubai, so she could see her best friend who lived out there. There wasn't anything I wouldn't do for Lauren. It's who I am, a loving, generous, caring person. I don't know any other way to be.

The first year of our relationship was perfect. We were best friends, soul mates, and wanted to see each other every day. I always remember having a conversation with my family about just how lovely Lauren is. She was like no one I'd ever met before. I distinctly remember saying to my family that Lauren would never hurt me. She just wasn't that type of a person. She's so soft and gentle. I thought to myself, I could not see myself without Lauren in my life, I wanted to be with her forever and I would do whatever it took to make that happen. We had connected and grown so close to one another, that it was impossible to separate from one another. However, there always comes a time when the balloon must be popped…What goes up must come down.
As they say, the honeymoon period was coming to an end.

Your true colours revealed

The first sign that things were not quite as they seemed was in December 2018. Two things occurred at this time. Lauren and her son, Sam moved into my four-bedroom detached property, which I owned at the time. So, there was plenty of room in the new-build property that I invested in. We set up Sam's room to how he would like it and I went out of my way to make them both feel very welcome in the next phase of our life together.

However, at the same time, I discovered an exciting opportunity to create a second stream of income that would provide us with more protection, financially. This was an opportunity to learn digital skills and master the art of becoming an affiliate marketer. This is where I promoted a company's products and services, without any previous experience, without being technical, without any qualification or pre-requisites. But most importantly, without having a big idea or having any products of my own. All that was needed was a laptop, an internet connection, and the commitment to do the work…I had all of that.

I was so excited about this and as soon as I mentioned it to Lauren, I could see that she was not impressed. She was completely against the idea of creating another source of income. I have no idea why. This is someone who did not work, and who claimed benefits from the government. No judgement, but I could not understand why she didn't get excited about this opportunity. It really was from this moment that our relationship just didn't feel the same anymore.

Regardless, I was on a mission to pursue this dream and commit to the process. I invested in myself, educated myself, and learned new, modern digital skills. I did not want to be relying on working for a large global company in a traditional 9-to-5 job my whole life, chasing paycheck to paycheck that was limited by a HR (human resources) department who did not know me nor my true worth. I also didn't want the worry, stress, and anxiety hanging over me about when my next job loss was going to come. I simply had to do this. I did not need any permission from anyone, except from myself. All I wanted was the love, respect, and support that I truly deserved…but Lauren was not prepared to give me this.

This was red flag #1…Why did I not do anything about this? …

So going into 2019, I was seeing more and more evidence that there was something fundamentally wrong with our relationship. Here are just some examples:

Lauren not letting me into her son's life the way I wanted. Even doing small things, like the school run on my own. She never wanted that.
Lauren told me on at least one occasion that I shouldn't be around children. Where on earth that came from, I have no idea.

Whenever we would have an argument or disagreement, Lauren would always punish me by ghosting or ignoring me for days, even weeks.

Lauren would always say that she couldn't commit to a relationship, but still wanted to be with me. So, it was giving me very mixed signals.
For some unknown reason, Lauren allowed her ex-partner, the father of her daughter, to live with her temporarily, while I was crying out to live with her. It was heartbreaking knowing he was in the house with her at night, not knowing what was going on. He always seemed to get priority over me. This was not jealousy. This was just far from a normal situation. I would never have my ex-partner live with me while I was in a relationship with someone else. To me, this was uncalled for and disrespectful. It showed a lack of compassion, love, and respect towards me, and I will never forget her doing this to me. To me, it was a form of cheating.

When Lauren would go into her shell and blank me, she would check into a place on Facebook and pretend to be with another man.

Lauren would never include me in activities, such as going to a kid's soft play area with her son, grandson, and niece. Oh yes, Lauren was a young grandmother. I never truly felt included in her family. I was always an outsider, someone who was invited to certain occasions and special events.

These were more rejections and red flags...Why did I not do anything about any of these?

Lauren and I discussed the possibility of investing in a property in Dubai. Since taking her there a few times by this point, we thought it would be such an amazing experience to look into living out there. So, I did some research and I booked an appointment to see a property sales team down in central London. I remember it was a Saturday morning and I drove down to London on my own from my house in Rugby, Warwickshire. This was when Lauren and Sam were living with me.

I spent about three hours getting into central London. It took me a while to find the place and then I spent no more than an hour in the appointment. They gave me lovely brochures to take away and have a look at. I really was excited about this. It took me about another three hours to drive home. But what happened when I walked in the door back home completely shocked me and made me so angry and hurt.

Not only did Lauren ignore what I had just done, but she also had a real go at me and was talking about things that she found on my electronic devices. Why on earth she thought she could look through my tablet while I was out doing a lovely thing for our future, I have no idea. I was so upset. We never did look through those brochures together. That dream was ruined as soon as I walked in the door. For me, this was another significant red flag in our relationship. But me being the loving me, just brushed it under the carpet and carried on.

Later that year, at my friend's wedding, more signs were starting to appear. I showed Lauren something on my phone and while my back was turned for five minutes, she was looking through my messages and then started questioning me about some of my conversations with other people...innocent and friendly conversations.

It got to a point towards the end of 2019 where I was getting fed up with Lauren's behaviour, and how I didn't feel loved at all. So over the Christmas period in 2019, we separated and took time apart. I was so upset and broken that I posted a video on YouTube sharing how I was being treated. I broke down with emotion while recording it. I was devastated and heartbroken...of course she had a go at me for posting this video. So, I removed it.

2020 was a new year and I was so excited and looking forward to my trip to the Gold Coast, Australia. I was going there to attend business and personal development workshops that I had invested in. Lauren and I were speaking again going into the new year. However, she did not accept my invitation to go on a trip of a lifetime with me. Again, she reminded me she didn't believe in what I was doing. Another red flag reminder.

Do you really think this little of me?

The most deceitful thing Lauren did to me when I got back from Australia was to invite her ex-partner to live with her for a few months, again. I'll never forget how it was all planned behind my back and then for her to say there was nothing wrong with it. I mean, who in their right mind would live with their ex-partner while in a relationship with someone else? I'm sorry, but this is not normal. It's unheard of and uncalled for. There are no words to explain this type of behaviour. This means while in a relationship with me, Lauren lived with her ex-partner on two separate occasions…yes…twice while in a relationship with me.

This certainly made me feel unloved, unwanted, and without a doubt…rejected. Just writing it now makes me feel sick. I asked myself again, why did I continue to participate in this toxic, disjointed, and broken relationship? I must have been so manipulated, but I loved her so much. Why Fran? you're probably wondering. Good question. I guess I had so much hope for us and I was prepared to keep fighting for us, even though it was just me wanting to win the cause.

In 2021, I reached out to one of my good friends from Australia. Miss G is someone who I connected with in 2020, at the same time the UK went into lockdown due to Covid. I worked with Miss G on a weight loss program for six months. She helped lose nearly nineteen kilograms in body fat in six months. It was an incredible experience.

Miss G is also a divine feminine essence and embodiment entrepreneur, who supports people to build connections with their intuition and authentic self, heal mind, body, soul, and consciously create life and relationships. So, for me, Miss G was the person I wanted to be around, supporting me, and guiding me on my new path in life. We worked together to improve my life and find that spark that I had lost. We had some powerful video zoom calls, and it was what I needed. Miss G gave me so much positive energy and a different perspective on life. I'll never forget when she shared a lovely heart-shaped plaque, which had the following words on it:

"You are focusing purely on the negative but there is also a positive side you are not seeing. Your mental attitude and thoughts can make things seem good or bad, beautiful or ugly. All is a matter of perception. What you think, you shall

become. Be positive, for behind the perceived darkness, there is much love, light, and good fortune."

I just love this and I'm extremely grateful for Miss G's support in all of this. This is an incredibly powerful and loving human being. All she wants is the best in everybody. That is all I want for people as well…to see the best in people and for them to realise their own potential that's hidden deep inside.

Miss G is the type of person who would never abandon or reject me. She is someone who is always there for me if I need her support. No matter what the problem. This is why I get to assess my circle of friends and evaluate anyone who no longer serves me, or is no longer aligned with my vision, if they're not, then they are removed. This is the only way I get to live a happy and fulfilled life, by surrounding myself with those who I can trust, who are 100% aligned with my vision, and who are always there to support me, with no judgement or criticism. Up until now, I welcomed everyone into my circle, which was the reason I was always getting hurt.

2022 was most definitely the start of the end of this broken relationship…I experienced four traumatic events because of Lauren's behaviour. After putting my house on the market in the summer of 2021, I finally managed to sell it and handed the keys over to the estate agency in February 2022. That was quite a surreal moment, as I had lived in that house for five years, to the day and it was where I was when I had met Lauren. We had so many great memories there. So, it was tough to walk away from that chapter in my life.

When I originally put the house on the market, I got a lot of abuse and criticism for selling my house. My family was outraged and could not believe what I was doing. I had family members call me when normally they wouldn't. I didn't know why I was being attacked. Well, that's what it felt like. I was told I was "reckless" and was "making a big mistake".

Why was I being treated like this? I could not understand it. I didn't get it. Is someone not allowed to sell their house these days? It felt like I needed to get approval from someone else. I have never and will never phone someone to say they are reckless for selling their house. If that's what they want to do, then that's their choice. It felt like my choices were always scrutinised, which made me so upset. It made me live my life like I needed approval, external validation, justification to do everything, even to breathe at times.

Lauren and I did finally agree that I would move into her place, so the three of us (including her son of course) could try again and make a fresh start. Maybe I was completely disillusioned, but everything appeared to be going to plan. It felt perfect. I was so happy that we were able to live together again...FINALLY. We were even speaking with kitchen and conservatory specialists, so we could do some nice work on Lauren's house to extend it with a brand new kitchen. It was such an exciting time, well, at least I thought it was.

Fran, Get out of my house

Then all of a sudden, Lauren turned again (Trauma #1 of 4). She never wanted to hang out or spend time with me and was always rushing out of the house. It was like she was sick of the sight of me. She then took it to a whole new level when she started reading my personal notebook and going through my laptop, while I was out with friends. And it was when I was out with a friend, she texted me in anger and rage, saying I was to move out. She was literally packing my things and putting them by the front door. She was completely out of control. I got back that evening to find my things by the door. I could not process what was going on. This was about eight weeks after I had moved in. It made no sense to me. She was so aggressive and accused me of planning to move out to Australia to be with Miss G, whom I mentioned earlier. I mean…really?…

I was again devastated and broken by Lauren's cold and malicious actions. I had a matter of days to find somewhere else to live, so I decided to move up to Liverpool. I had no family or connections there, so no doubt it was going to be a challenge for me. Well, I managed to do it. I found a one-bedroom apartment in the centre of the city. It had such an amazing view of Albert Docks. However, this was not the view that I had in my vision. But somehow, I had to adapt to being on my own, without Lauren in my life.

I did my best to keep busy. I joined a social app called meetup, which introduced me to a lovely group of young people, who were just out having fun and enjoying themselves. So, I connected with people and built up my circle of friends very quickly that way. The hurt, pain, and suffering inside me was still so fresh and was eating me up inside.

I simply had to keep focused on my new vision, keep busy, and be around people who cared about me, and who loved me for who I was. I went for long walks every day, I went to the gym regularly, and I chatted with so many nice people, including the personal trainers at a local gym. They even gave me their phone number and said to call them anytime if I ever wanted a chat. I would never have got that support from Lauren. The more I think about it, the more I realise just how little she was there for me. She was in her own little critical and judgemental bubble. I never felt rejected while living in Liverpool. The only thing that was rejecting me up until this point was myself. My decisions and choices created this lifestyle for myself, and I had no one else to blame but myself.

And did I learn from my mistakes? Of course not. Lauren managed to manipulate me once again and crawl back into my life. I honestly don't know why I allowed myself to do this. I said that I would raise my standards by setting new boundaries for myself. This was to protect me, my mental and physical well-being. Lauren visited me a couple of times, and we had lovely weekends. It was like nothing negative had ever happened between us. We went for walks, had lovely meals together, kissed and cuddled. It was perfect…but of course, it was an illusion.

Fran, I have a surprise for you

However, Lauren seemed to turn yet again (Trauma #2 of 4). This time it was on Monday, the 1st of August 2022. I will never forget it. I had just got back from my lovely morning walk and as I entered my apartment, I messaged Lauren on WhatsApp just to tell her I was out for my walk and that I love, and I miss her. Her reply completely broke my world. I could not believe what I was reading. She replied:

"I don't love you Fran and I want to see other people."

I nearly collapsed to the floor with all of the pain inside me. I was devastated. I was heartbroken. It felt like Lauren had ripped out my heart and stabbed it over and over again with a knife, and then stabbed me in the back repeatedly with the same knife. That probably doesn't even come close to how it felt. Honestly, I was broken beyond belief. I was shocked and felt sick.

Somehow, I kept going. I told my family what had just happened. I could not concentrate or focus on anything; I could hardly eat or sleep. My mind just kept going around in circles, asking so many questions:

"Why has she done this to me?" "What have I done wrong?" "Why is she taking it out on me and no one else?", "I don't get it, I don't understand it" "Why is she so horrible to me?" ...

I will never forget this time in my life, when I was living on the ninth-floor apartment, above a hotel in the centre of Liverpool and I thought to myself, "I just want this pain to go away." It was an intolerable amount of pain, and the quickest way for me to do that was to walk up to my floor-to-ceiling window, open it up, take one last deep breath, and just lean forward. Gravity would take care of the rest. It would be over very quickly, and the pain would be gone. Fortunately, due to the safety window, this was not possible. But this was what I was thinking. Instead, I decided to put a post on Facebook. This was a cry out for help. I didn't know what else to do. I had to share my feelings with my loved ones, as I didn't want to face this alone.

"I'm trying my best in life but it feels like I don't wanna be here anymore. I have let everyone down. My family, my kids, my relationships."

Here are some of the lovely feedback that I received when I posted my pain and suffering on Facebook, despite the fact I wasn't expecting any comments.

"Hi Fran, thinking of you and wishing you all the best. Remember you are tremendously gifted and extremely talented in this space. Keep crankin' along man. Here for you as needed and happy to chat any time too."
"Fran, your family and kids love you so much. We all feel like we let people down now and again, but as you said you are trying your best, and that's all we

can do! Just take one day at a time. You got this!!! Take time to play with your kids and they will lift your spirits up. Sending you lots of hugs"

"Thinking of you bud, bad times pass, reach out to family and support, and never be afraid to ask for help, you're a really good person and you will get through this, we get tested all the time with difficult situations in life, get through today and tomorrow will be better, thinking of you"

"All storms pass mate. You've got a massive heart. It might not feel like it but I can guarantee your family loves you and needs you despite what might be going on. You've got support, you're not alone."

"Fran, it doesn't feel like it right now, but this feeling will pass, impossible as that may seem. Life can be very hard sometimes and if we can try and just weather those storms and trust there are better days ahead. Please be gentle and kind to your precious self. You are an incredible and kind human being."

"Fran, one day, you will tell your story of how you overcame what you went through, and it will be someone else's survival guide. You've got this mate. Always reach out. I'm here for you."

"Fran it is so brave to say you are struggling. Deep breath and hope tomorrow is a better day, sending positive thoughts and love"

"You can overcome this; you are stronger than you know. You have taken the first step; everybody is supporting you. You can do this"

"You feel like that because you're so detached from your inner being. Life is supposed to be joyful and the world we've grown up in tells us otherwise. You haven't let anyone down - you are on a journey to connect more with who you truly are - leaving the human crap as just that. This is a learning opportunity for you and when you move past this you will have grown 1000%. Be kind to yourself. x"

Wow, I could not believe the level of support I received from this one comment I had posted on Facebook. This feedback gave me more confidence and belief in myself that I was worthy, I did matter, and I had a purpose in life. I am loved by so many people, and I get to acknowledge that. I acknowledge that I am not alone…If you're reading this, and you feel like you're alone, you're trapped, and you don't know how to get out of this dark place, let me tell you this. You are not alone…You'll never walk alone. I am here for you. This is my mission…to provide people with the belief and hope that what you may think is impossible, is in fact possible.

I simply could not figure out why I was allowing these experiences to happen to me, but I had to keep pushing forward through the pain and suffering. I continued to attend business networking events, and the next event I went to, the timing was perfect. I met a lovely young, enthusiastic business innovator, and entrepreneur, John. Like me, John had just been through a similar situation where his long-term relationship, with the love of his life, had unfortunately come to an end. We agreed to hold each other high and that's what we did. We became best mates and inseparable. John certainly has more strength and willpower to get through difficult times like this.

Whereas I'm more sensitive, and emotional. I hated people walking away from me. The pain became too unbearable for me. I didn't know how to handle it or manage my emotions organically. Thankfully John was there to support me every step of the way. I even joined the same gym. We had some good sessions together and I got to chat with so many other lovely people. They were all so incredibly supportive. However, I did have some very difficult emotional moments when I was in the gym. There was one occasion when I was sitting in the sauna for about an hour. I broke down in tears as the pain was still at the surface. I took this photo just as I came out of the sauna. I don't know what came over me, but I had a huge number of emotions that needed releasing. The pain from Lauren was still there.

I now had time to reflect on my life, what I wanted, what my new vision looked like. So, I made the bold decision to move back down to the south coast, to live closer to my girls, Faye and Sara.

Fran, I'm going to give you the silent treatment now

My biggest fear was for Faye and Sara to reject me as well. I didn't want to be a failed father. I didn't want them to be disappointed in me for not being there for them. I want them to love me for who I am, and tell all of their friends about me, about the success I'm creating in life. I want them to be proud of me. I want them to be my biggest fans. I want to be the best dad to them and not be another statistic of a father walking out on their children… abandoning them. No way, that's certainly not me or who I am. I am a loving, caring father, who will do whatever it takes to protect my children.

During this time, Lauren again does what she does best…blank me from her life (Trauma #3 of 4). This time it was in November 2022, when I flew to Florida to attend another business event and catch up with some friends. Again, Lauren turned down this trip to support me. I won't go into detail about the trip, but I'll never forget the last video WhatsApp call I made with Lauren before I flew back to Manchester airport. It was Tuesday, the 22nd of November, 2022 and I was sitting in Jacksonville airport in Florida, a little bit stressed after driving to the airport and getting through security.

I got a large bottle of water, sat down, and was looking forward to having a nice conversation with her. I was so excited about seeing Lauren on Thursday, giving her a huge hug and kiss (and her gift of course!). The conversation went well. It seemed to be a perfectly normal conversation. Nothing out of the ordinary. We were discussing whether I would move back into her property and give it another go.

I boarded that plane with a smile on my face, thinking everything was okay. Not knowing what Lauren was thinking, I had no idea that she was again about to break my world into millions of pieces. It wasn't until I landed back in Manchester airport the following morning that I found out the real truth of who Lauren really was. I was super excited to see Lauren the next day (Thursday) and had planned to get on the train and visit her and her family for a few days.

I met up with John for a drink that Wednesday afternoon. Everything was perfect. Then the phone vibrated. It was a message from Lauren…My world felt like it was over… Again. My heart was ripped apart by what I read…

"I can't be with someone who is careless with their money, what have you got to show for the money, no house, no car, sorry but it's true.
I can't support what you're doing, sorry.
It's not going to work you moving here,
unless you have a job.
Do not ask me to put money in anything again.
You want to move in now you're skint and want me to put money into a scam."

What can I say…I was devastated yet again. Wait, there is more.

In December 2022, I discovered that Lauren had been stealing funds that I was supposed to be paid. Long story short, when we briefly lived together in Lauren's place for eight weeks, we had a joint benefits claim set up. This was after another job loss, and Lauren was not working by choice. After she kicked me out for no reason, we changed this to a single claim. Unfortunately, my claim was linked to Lauren's bank details.

This happened in May that year.

So, it was set up like this for many months. I just never noticed it. However, when I realised and kindly confronted Lauren about this, she coldly refused to return the funds to me. She knew perfectly well that it was not hers and she was not entitled to that money. It was approximately five and a half thousand pounds and Lauren simply refused to transfer it over to me. Instead, she reluctantly paid my three hundred pounds and then said, "Do not message me again."

This was now becoming a pattern and a game for Lauren to play. I was lost for words. I was losing all hope in fighting for this relationship, which at best, was broken. It was so toxic that I could no longer process the logic. Was there any sense to it? I was completely shocked and stunned and didn't know what to do. I felt like her behaviour was abusive, manipulative and controlling. What gave her the right to attack me for being ambitious, courageous, and brave for stepping into the path of a new and exciting career that was going to give her everything she ever wanted?

Lauren told me so many times the things she wanted, the lifestyle she desired, a nice big house, a lovely car, a nice family and romantic holidays, pampering days, and spa weekends. She wanted so many nice things, including an engagement ring. I don't know how many times we discussed rings. We would always look at them when looking around the shops. She even had her engagement ring finger measured twice when we were together. Once, within two months of meeting each other, as I mentioned, and the second time was during the Covid pandemic. So to me, she wanted to marry me, in hindsight, perhaps it was just part of her game?

I had signed up to be a volunteer at the brain charity, which helps with every neurological condition, including Lauren's frontal lobe damage. I did this because of her story and because I loved her. She never once acknowledged that gesture. I even offered to invest my time, finances and efforts in a special education needs (SEN) community centre for her son. I said I would invest in a facility that was for sale, or possibly design and build the building from scratch. I was so excited about the project, as I'm passionate about supporting children with learning difficulties. I was already designing the layout of the community centre in my head. My vision for her son was to build a lasting legacy for him that everyone could be proud of. I made this incredible gesture to Lauren on a number of occasions. How do you think she reacted? You guessed it. She never acknowledged or showed any sign of gratitude. To be honest, it was very hurtful that she chose not to even recognise the efforts I was going to in order to build a lasting future and legacy for her child. This is the type of person she is, which is such a shame. I guess the reason I fought for the relationship for so long was because I saw potential in her…in us.

I'd always hoped to provide all those things for her. That's what love is. However, I don't recognise who she is anymore. I'm not here to judge, and I don't ever want to criticise anyone behind their back, but there is only so much selfish and ungrateful behaviour I can take. It's so uncalled for and completely disrespectful. I don't deserve that after everything I've done for her after all those years being together.

Lauren destroyed my life on at least three separate occasions in 2022 and she seemed to get a thrill out of punishing me for weeks and months at a time, where she simply turned cold, didn't answer my calls, wasn't interested in engaging in anything I did, never asked how my family were doing or wanted to interact with them.

I reflected back on my life in 2022, and I journaled some of my experiences. Here is what I wrote…

"It's 04:38am in the morning on New Year's Eve (two days before New Years Day) and I'm reflecting on what a year it's been. I don't think I can process what has happened, but I'll start to dissect it and I'll try to make some sense out of it.

It all started in Rugby, Warwickshire when I was about to sell my lovely four-bedroom detached house. I simply didn't feel connected with the area, I felt isolated, especially coming out of lockdown. I just felt it was time to move on from there.

My plan was to hit the reset button on my life, invest some of the equity into my business by investing in me and just create real success. My ideal scenario would be to live with my partner at the time, Lauren and just live a simple, happy life.

I then started to look at Liverpool and I started the process of submitting an application for a rental property. Long story short, Lauren could see I was about to move on without her and said she'd be heart-broken if I moved to Liverpool on my own. So I cancelled the application and we both agreed that I'd live with her and her son.

It was on the 24th February, 2022 that I moved all of my things down to her place.

I felt so happy. I finally realised that we could rebuild our relationship and to finally move on and be happy together.

I took Lauren, her sister, and her niece to Dubai for a lovely family holiday. It was perfect. Although I couldn't really switch off from work, and be completely present with the girls. I had a couple of moments when I was stressed and took it out on the girls, but I wasn't aggressive. Just a bit snappy. We're all human, we all do it. However, with Lauren, she doesn't let you forget about these things. She punishes you for weeks and months for no reason.

On the flight back, Lauren and her sister thanked me for the holiday (how genuine they were I don't know) and they said they would treat me to a massage when we got home. Did I ever get the massage? Of course not. It was a load of lies and false promises.

The relationship between myself and Lauren then seemed to deteriorate rapidly, even though I paid off her credit card (three thousand pounds). This is just who I am. Thinking of others before myself.

I'll never forget when we were out for dinner (the four of us again) and we were planning the next family holiday. This time I wanted to include my two girls, Faye and Sara. I have no idea what possessed Lauren to then decide to exclude my girls from the holiday. I was so angry, and I couldn't understand her actions. She actually manipulated me and the situation, as if I had done something wrong. I was so angry with her and what she had done. She felt she had to be in control, with no respect for my feelings at all. How could someone not include their partner's children in a family holiday? Again, my experience of Lauren was selfish, disrespectful.

Anyway, things got worse from there. Lauren was going through my things, going through my laptop, reading my journal, looking at messages on my Facebook messenger. She had no trust or respect for me anymore.

In mid-April 2022, when I was out with my friend having a few beers, Lauren texted me saying I was to move out. She was even chucking all of my things by her front door. Her behaviour became so erratic and aggressive. I couldn't get my head round what was going on.

So, I had about a week or two to find somewhere. I decided to move to Liverpool, and I very quickly found a place. I used the exact same removal company (the same one I had used only a couple of months earlier to move my things into Lauren's place) to take my things up to Liverpool. I'll never forget it, the van dropped me to the train station and I got the train up on my own and met the van at my new place. This was because of insurance purposes.

So I started my life again in Liverpool, feeling completely broken and empty inside. Even to this day, I don't know why she kicked me out and I guess I never will.

The relationship between myself and Lauren continued, but it was never the same again.

In August, she randomly said she no longer loved me or wanted to see me. She had lost all love and respect for me.

As my biggest passion is motorsport, Lauren kindly agreed to attend Brands Hatch race track with me to watch the last round of the British Superbikes in mid October, 2022. She knew this was my thing, and like five years earlier, she came with me. I said to her, this time was actually better than the first time we went. We had a perfect weekend, shopping in BlueWater shopping centre, getting ideas for Christmas gifts. The race day on the Sunday was like a hot summer's day. It was perfect. I fell in love with Lauren again. I didn't want this moment to end. We also booked some hotel rooms to have a lovely Christmas together and planned to do some Christmas shopping and spend time with my girls in Dorset. It sounded perfect.

Things were okay between us when I was in Florida, but by the time I landed back in Manchester, Lauren no longer wanted to be with me. She cancelled all of our plans, including the Christmas ice ball with The Brain Charity. This was it, this was the real Lauren coming out and finally she was revealing her true colours.

So, I now have to come to terms with what has happened this year with the relationship and just accept it. I want answers, but I'll never get them.

I've learned that I cannot be in a relationship with someone who has an unpredictable, hot and cold personality. No matter what I say or do, it's never good enough. It's exhausting, mentally and emotionally draining."

So can you see how messed up my head was from the mixed signals?

Hot and cold from her all the time. This was how it was for over four years. I don't need someone like that in my life. I deserve better. But, did I learn from my mistakes? Of course not!

Fran, I want to marry you…Oh wait, no I don't

It was around the end of January, early February 2023 when I started receiving WhatsApp messages again from Lauren. This was after three months of her ignoring me and blanking me from her life. She didn't want to know me over Christmas 2022. I had never felt so rejected, hollow and empty. My family could see just how broken I was that Christmas.

Lauren's message frequency was around once a week. The first one I received was when I was on my way back from visiting my daughters, Faye and Sara. This trip was so I could tell them about moving back down, so I could be closer to them. It was Saturday, the 14th of January, 2023 and it took me around thirteen hours to get down to Faye and Sara. I met them for two hours for dinner, which was amazing. I then stayed the night in the hotel and then made a nine-hour coach journey back up to Liverpool. And it was while on this coach, I received a message from Lauren, "Hi how are you?" I did not reply until the following evening.

There was so much going on in my life. It's hard to put it into words. I was in the process of relocating from Liverpool to Poole in Dorset, to live closer to Faye and Sara. I was in the middle of a life transformation and leadership program, which was really stretching and challenging me more than ever before. And now, my long-term partner of five years was talking to me again, after walking away from me for three months, just before Christmas. I was very sensitive to every little thing. Anything and everything triggered my emotions and I often broke down very easily.

Lauren agreed to bring her son up to Liverpool so we could all catch up and spend some quality time together. I was really looking forward to that, but I had lost so much confidence in relationships…in Lauren. So I was cautious and wary, determined not to let her hurt me again. Things were great. Lauren even supported me with the house move, which I was very grateful for. I was just approaching my 40th birthday (1st of March) and I couldn't believe I was about to hit this milestone.

The relationship with Lauren couldn't be better and we were closer than ever. Lauren admitted she made a mistake by leaving me and promised that she would never ever do that again. Lauren was immediately considering moving down to Poole to be with me forever. We were even talking about getting engaged and buying a house together. My life felt great and I felt complete again with Lauren back in my life. It felt like a fresh start, something I had been dreaming about for so many years. However, this dream, as you guessed it, was shattered again. Lauren walked away from me, yet again.

Fran, how could you let this happen again, you're probably asking? … I know how could I, it tallied up to Trauma #4 of 4. Not to mention all of the other times she hurt me.

It was the weekend of the 24th of March 2023, Lauren and her son came down to visit me in Poole. It was incredible. We had the best time. I was on cloud nine. That Saturday night, we met up with my daughters, Faye and Sara and all had dinner together in the local hotel, where myself and Lauren used to stay. We took some lovely photos, and it truly was perfect. The feeling I had inside was pure happiness.

The weekend was perfect, with walks on the beach and other happy memories being created. Unfortunately, as always, the weekend is never long enough and Lauren had to drive back home. I was still very happy knowing I would see them very soon. I'll never forget giving Sam (her son), a cup of ice for the drive home, as he loves to suck on ice cubes. I also gave Lauren a loving kiss in the car before they drove home. I was so happy inside, but little did I know this would be the last time I saw them both. I had no idea that Lauren was about to break my heart again... This time it would be permanent.

The cold, callous, and defensive barriers came up once again from Lauren. She didn't tell me, but I could tell from Sam that the reason they were leaving early that Sunday morning was to meet up with Lauren's daughter's father, the same person Lauren allowed to live with her twice during our relationship. I didn't really think anything of it that day, but I was shocked, heartbroken, confused, and angry when she went cold on me again. She blanked me in the same way she had done over the years when she didn't want to be around me. I could not believe that I was experiencing this same behaviour, AGAIN.

I sat down on Easter Monday to reflect on what happened over the last few days. It was a very tough and to be honest, a lonely Easter. I was still trying to process what had happened and yet again it had to do with the most toxic relationship I've ever experienced. In a matter of hours after having the best weekend, I found myself being stabbed in the back, my heart ripped out of my chest and destroyed, and was left feeling emotionally abused and bullied. I was significantly traumatised at this point. My mind could not process this anymore. The pain and unworthy feeling was too unbearable. Once again, I felt like giving up on life…I felt like tapping out. It had to be the quickest way to get rid of this pain. But as always, I could never go through with it.

For some unknown reason, Lauren, AGAIN decided to dump me. I know I have myself to blame, but I asked her over and over again, what she did to me over Christmas destroyed me and that she was never to do that to me ever again. She promised she would never do it again. In fact, I was so clingy and kept seeking reassurance that we could finally start to rebuild our relationship. I just could not figure it out. I simply had no way to process what was going on. When Lauren visited me, she gave me a tiny artificial plant with a message on the side of it that said, *"I'll forever be your always"*, and a gorgeous, personalised birthday card with photos of us on it. Some great memories we created together (including moments towards the end of our relationship). However, that artificial plant should have said:

"I'll pretend to love you for the next three weeks, and then I'll break your heart again".

I'm realising now, enough is enough

Within a matter of hours, she completely changed her personality. The true Lauren was finally being revealed. She turned into her cold, nasty, horrible… evil side. I know that may sound harsh, but she was pure evil. I didn't understand how she could flip like a light switch and remove all emotions. She had no regard for my feelings and did only what pleased her and what was convenient. She even accused me of being narcissistic. I was completely shocked, I nearly collapsed in the street when she texted me this. I tried to call her straight away after reading that message, but knowing Lauren, she refused to speak to me. She wouldn't answer my call.

So again, I had to pick myself up. Now, all hope for saving this relationship had gone. I no longer trusted her and the hurt and pain was unbearable, as I had done absolutely nothing wrong to deserve that. If anything, I loved her more than anyone possibly could. Her behaviour was just shocking and inexplicable. It was not love; it was the complete opposite. But I was doing my best to stay focused on my vision and future, which no longer included her in it. I realised I couldn't save her.

And it continued…

I reached out to her after a week of not speaking to one another. Her reply was devastating and completely ripped my heart out. She wrote, *"Sorry Fran but I'm seeing someone."* I replied *"What?? How could you do this to me?"* Lauren replied *"Just delete me."*

I never felt so empty, unwanted, and unloved. My world completely fell apart, AGAIN and I knew this was the end. It had to be the end…enough was enough. She blocked me immediately on WhatsApp, I replied *"You're horrible and fake."* Of course, this was the rage and anger talking. I didn't mean to say that. It just came out. I was full of anger and I was hurting so badly. It's hard to put into words how upset I was. Within minutes, we were talking on Facebook Messenger, but it was so cold. I ended the conversation but wished her a nice day and for her son to have a great week back in school after the Easter break.

Later that afternoon, she removed me from Facebook and blocked me. So, to me, Lauren certainly did not love me and this inexplicable behaviour demonstrated her true colours. We did eventually speak again. However, it felt so different from the Lauren I fell in love with. From my experience, for nearly six years she said she loved me, wanted to marry me, but didn't want me in her house anymore…that she didn't love her other ex (her daughter's dad), but is happy to have him to live with her, months at a time…It made no sense.

I was always clinging onto that last ounce of hope that maybe one day we could be together again, finally work it out, and live happily ever after. I wanted that more than anything. She destroyed those dreams on her own. I could not have loved her and supported her anymore. I had exhausted all of my love and energy for her. I sacrificed so much for this person, and this was the thanks I got.

A man's perspective: Saying "NO" to domestic abuse

I have been through so much domestic abuse, and it does finally break you. The reason I eventually came around to actively seeking help, was because being in a relationship for over five years with domestic abuse was too much for me. It can be too much for so many people. It's so highly taboo to discuss domestic abuse among men. Staggeringly, so many men feel like they're weak for being dominated and controlled by a woman.

Some men feel that with domestic violence being so prevalent among women, they should mute their experiences. And sometimes, it has nothing to do with gender, because it's still abuse. The feelings of shame, worthlessness, lack of confidence and fear can circle a man, like it can a woman. This is a big topic, and I know there is so much more to it than this. But I feel like it is my role as the author of this book to share some information that may help you.

Being in an abusive relationship tipped me over the edge, and I didn't realise the negative impact it had on my wellbeing.

I want to be clear on the common forms of domestic abuse and provide you with the awareness of what to look out for. I'll share with you what I experienced personally in this relationship. I'll put a [Yes] beside the ones that I have personally experienced. These lists cover only some of the items, so you may experience many more. This is just to remind you how you may be treated.

Emotional Abuse
Belittle you, or put you down? **[Yes]**
Blame you for the abuse or arguments? **[Yes]**
Deny that abuse is happening, or downplay it? **[Yes]**
Gaslight you? **[Yes]**
Isolate you from your family and friends? **[Yes]**
Stop you going to college or work?
Make unreasonable demands for your attention?
Accuse you of flirting or having affairs? **[Yes]**
Tell you what to wear, who to see, where to go, and what to think?
Control your money, or not give you enough to buy food or other essential things?
Monitor your social media profiles, share photos or videos of you without your consent or use GPS locators to know where you are? **[Yes]**

Threats and Intimidation
Threaten to hurt or kill you?
Destroy things that belong to you?
Stand over you, invade your personal space? **[Yes]**

Threaten to kill themselves or the children?
Read your emails, texts or letters? **[Yes]**
Harass or follow you? **[Yes]**

Physical Abuse

Slap, hit or punch you?
Push or shove you?
Bite or kick you?
Burn you?
Choke you or hold you down?
Throw things?

Sexual Abuse

Touch you in a way you do not want to be touched?
Make unwanted sexual demands?
Hurt you during sex?
Pressure you to have unsafe sex – for example, not using a condom?
Pressure you to have sex?

Financial Abuse

Inflicting physical harm or injury that would prevent you from attending work?
Harassing you at your workplace?
Controlling financial assets and effectively putting you on an allowance?
Damaging your credit score?
Not supporting you in your career development? **[Yes]**
Not supporting you in new financial opportunities (Assets)? **[Yes]**
Steal money from you? **[Yes]**

Have I been loving a narcissist all this time?

Being in a toxic relationship really did send me over the edge. I don't mean she just gave me a slight tap to tip me over, she absolutely obliterated me for over four years. As you can see, I experienced much of the abuse I listed above. It was an Oscar performance from my ex-partner. It was all an act. What made this so hard to process in my mind was that no one else could see it. Narcissists are so clear, calculated, and clever in how they play you. Unfortunately, society tends to associate men with being narcissists. That's not the case. Some women can be just as abusive and violent as some men.

It took me over five years to realise I loved someone whom I believed was a narcissist. That's just my opinion. For me, the penny dropped the day she called ME a narcissist. This is because they are so clever at how they play with your mind. My point is that men are not always the perpetrators. A lot of the time, men are the victims. But again, it's okay to talk about it, it's okay to be full of emotions. It takes a long time to heal from narcissistic abuse. It is a form of trauma, and yes, I believe I was healing from PTSD that this person caused me. It's devastating and it destroys your soul, your spirit, your confidence and who you stand for.

This is in no way meant to be judgemental. This is my own neutral opinion of Lauren, who I have known and loved since the day I first met her in August 2017. Even before we met for the first time, I was already falling for her. She had that impact. I am now simply sharing my experience of Lauren after six years and the reasons why things became too difficult to sustain our relationship. These few words do not come close to the pain, suffering, and mental trauma that Lauren has caused me over the years.

It took me nearly six years to realise that I was in love with someone with a narcissistic personality. I was in a cluster B personality disorder relationship. I have been advised and seen video footage of narcissistic behaviour. What I experienced personally was remarkably similar to these videos. I am not here to judge or criticise Lauren or anyone in life, but one question I feel like asking at this moment in time is…

"How did I fall in love with a narcissist?"

At the end of our relationship, I was so traumatised, I didn't know what to do. I was rock bottom. It felt like I had lost all of my confidence, the happy, cheerful person I used to be just didn't exist anymore. I didn't know who I was. I didn't know who I'd become, as I had lost my identity. All of my boundaries were destroyed. Lauren thought she could turn love on and off like a light switch or the television, when it was convenient for her in life. It's just who she is and no one can change that, only herself.

Each time Lauren disrespected me in this traumatising way, my mind and body would default to a paralysed state. It was as if my entire body had gone into a limp home mode, just like your car does when it senses a fault with one or multiple systems. Your car does what it can to protect itself from further damage, hence, it allows you to carefully get home. And that's what my body was doing to me. It wouldn't allow me to function correctly with this diagnosis of pain. It was trying to protect me. However, my limp home mode was not the solution for me…I had to overcome being paralysed because of one person. I chose not to live my life on Lauren's terms anymore. Firstly, I shifted my mindset and raised my standards, which included setting new boundaries for myself.

Like I say, I'm not here to judge anyone, especially Lauren, who was the love of my life, the person who I wanted to be with forever. Even to this day, I will always love her and her family. Similarly, I respect her decisions in life. I just wish she recognised what she did to me, the pain she caused, what she has lost, and what could have been. I wish her all the best and I hope she finds the happiness that she deserves.

It's time for change. New boundaries have been set and new standards have been created. I get to choose new ground rules. From the first day we spoke to this current day, I have always seen so much potential in Lauren, and I have done everything in my power to support her and unleash this brilliance that I know is within her. However, hurt people hurt people, and the only way for Lauren to find her power is to do it herself, as opposed to projecting her pain onto other people...the people who love her and care about her the most.

"I did my absolute best for you, Lauren, but did you ever really know me?"...

And that is what I have been doing with my life...pleasing other people. All of this hurt, pain and suffering caused by other people, controlling, manipulating, bullying me... *"It ends now."*. It's time to unleash my own power within. I can certainly hold my head high knowing I did my absolute best for Lauren and I'm doing my best in life, with the best intentions. I am proud of who I am. I want to be accepted for who I am, and simply loved for who I am (unconditionally). I accept everyone else for who they are. All I ask is for the same in return. I don't ask for much. I can only be my powerful, authentic, loving self, and this is who I get to be.

Do you resonate with any of this? Have you experienced or currently going through something similar? Well, know this. You're not alone.

Small nudges trigger big changes

Since this toxic and abusive relationship, I went through a period of getting emotional and teary-eyed by the smallest of things. For example, watching a professional motorbike rider crashing in the last race of the season and not winning the championship title. I never used to break down watching this sort of thing. Even when I listened to certain songs, I became an emotional mess. The trauma of being the victim in the most toxic relationship has huge side effects and takes very little to trigger these emotions. So, if you're a man reading this, and you feel you're in a similar situation, know that this is normal.

There is nothing to worry about.
This will pass.
You will get through this.
Reach out for support, reach out to me.
We are all here for you.
You're not alone.

The mind-map everyone needs to 'Boundary-ville' and 'Casa Del Limitations'

Having experienced so much rejection and trauma in my life, I thought I would analyse this further and understand what was going on and why I continued to get the same outcome, regardless of the situation. So, the first thing I looked at is what things I would say to people with NO limitations or boundaries. In other words, how I have been living my whole life. Here is what I discovered I was constantly saying to people:

"I'll do that for you."
"Do you want to go for dinner? I'll pay for it."

"Let me pay off your credit card."
"Let me book a holiday for us."
"Don't worry, I'll get it."
"I'll drive us there."
"I'm always here if you need a chat."
"Why are you not talking to me? I've done nothing wrong."
"Do you want to do X?"
"Do you want to go to Z?"
"Anything I can do to help?"
"You're welcome to stay at my place."
"Do you want me to come over and mind him/chat?"
"Do you want me to do anything for you?"
"Do you want me to pick up anything while I'm out?"
"Do you want me to go out and get you anything?"
"Do you want me to pick you up?"
"I'll drop you home."
"I got you a little gift."
"I don't want to upset anyone."
"Of course, no problem."
"Do you want me to get a new job where you live?"

Then, it dawned on me: Am I really a people pleaser? I always just thought it was the right thing to do - be nice to others. Nice, but in a different way, and this is part of my transformation journey. I have designed a whole new set of boundaries and limitations for myself, which can be found in Chapter 8 and in strategies #25 and #26 of Chapter 9.

CHAPTER EIGHT

THE 145 HOUR ZOOM CALL

Welcome to leadership and mindset transformation

One of the methods that I used to overcome this trauma of an intimate relationship, and every other difficult experience in my life, was to invest in a world-leading transformational leadership program.

This program not only transformed my life, but it also transformed the lives of so many people around the world. It has two main components - leadership and mindset transformation - which form the foundation of its success. At its core, it is an interactive way to become aware of our own patterns of behaviour, unlearn what isn't working, and create new ways of thinking that bring out our fullest potential.

On a personal level, this program helped me make sense of the changes I had experienced as a result of the traumatic events in my life, such as my intimate relationships, job losses and personal abandonments. It taught me how to create new perspectives by connecting with my feelings, rather than staying stuck in a victimhood or anger mindset. I gained valuable insight into why certain patterns kept repeating themselves in my relationships and how I could shift them for the better. I was able to start making conscious changes in both my outer world, as well as my inner self, which involved setting new boundaries and new personal standards. This was about self-love and self-respect that I did not truly have before I started this program.

In addition to providing individual support for personal growth, the program also had a strong focus on collective learning that encouraged participants to connect with others who were going through similar experiences. We learned from each other's stories, while helping each other heal from various traumas in our lives - something no one should have to do alone. This created supportive lifelong friendships within the group and was a powerful reminder that we are never really alone even in moments filled with pain and suffering.

The transformational leadership program has been incredibly successful, due to its ability to empower people from all walks of life around the world with the confidence, strength, courage and resilience needed to overcome their toughest challenges yet turn their dreams into reality. By combining leadership training with personal development tools, such as mindset shift techniques, this program gives individuals an opportunity to tap into their inner resources for self-transformation and ultimately live their most fulfilled lives possible! I'll share with you my personal experiences during this four-month program. Firstly, my team was known as HCL40.

The program was over a four-month period, split into three phases: Vision, Breakthrough and Practice. There were thirteen video zoom calls, each lasting approximately twelve hours. For me, this was throughout the night. Yes, it was very intensive but very rewarding.

Phase 1: Vision – *"Develop a fresh canvas on which to create your most amazing life. Create a vision that is far beyond what you believe is possible right now and prepare yourself to do your best work in the world."*

Phase 2: Breakthrough – *"Redefine your life's vision and put the pieces in place to begin living it. This is where you'll learn to transform your limiting beliefs and break through fear-based barriers to create the life you truly want. You'll develop "external" skills like time management, goal setting, and effective communication, and "internal" processes like self-love, empowering others, and breaking through your fears."*

Phase 3: Practice – *"This is where you become a kickass finisher. This is where you get stuff done. You'll lock in all the work you've done so far, so it sticks… so you can LIVE the strategic plan you've developed."*

I had the chance to hit reset on my life and release what had been holding me back from having the impact and life I crave. This program left me with so much energy and commitment to follow through on my biggest life vision.

Here are my new ground rules in life

I learned so much about ground rules. I came to the awareness with an understanding of the importance of ground rules in the context of leadership. Ground rules are guidelines that help to keep individuals and teams focused, organised and motivated. In addition to providing a sense of structure and control, properly enforced ground rules help foster an atmosphere of trust and respect within teams.

When it comes to creating effective ground rules for a team, there are various approaches leaders can and should take. One common approach is for all team members to follow an induction process, where they are clearly informed of all the rules within the organisation, or program, so they are on the same page.

Another common approach is to involve members of the team in the process by asking them for their input on what they believe should be included. This helps ensure that everyone is on board with the rules and understands their purpose. It also promotes ownership among team members and encourages collaboration, as everyone works together towards a common goal or set of expectations. Additionally, when implementing ground rules, leaders should make sure they remain consistent and enforce them fairly across all members.

To ensure that ground rules are implemented effectively, leaders must first have a clear idea of what their desired outcomes are for the group or project they are leading. Once these goals have been established, it is important for leaders to communicate these goals clearly to their team members. Once goals have been communicated, leaders should then discuss how best to implement ground rules in order to reach those desired outcomes effectively, while also taking into consideration any potential obstacles or challenges involved along the way.

The success of any group depends on how well its members adhere to its established ground rules. To reinforce adherence amongst its team members, a leader can use techniques such as rewards and recognition, when individuals abide by these guidelines, or take initiative with projects or tasks outside of their job descriptions. This encourages other team members to follow suit and reinforces positive behaviours within the group as a whole.

Overall, establishing and enforcing proper ground rules is essential when it comes to effective leadership in any organisation or project-based endeavour. By involving team members in the process from start to finish and recognising positive behaviours amongst them, when necessary, leaders can create an environment where productive collaboration can happen, while still ensuring progress is made towards achieving desired outcomes, efficiently and accurately.

This is exactly what I'm doing with my life to avoid the same type of rejection I have experienced. I am implementing new ground rules for myself personally. This means creating new boundaries, and higher standards in my life. That way I protect myself from more potential pain, and suffering. With new ground rules in place, I have better control over my life and who influences my personal circle.

The following new personal ground rules are an integral part of my future success and happiness:

I am a powerful, authentic, loving leader, and I always stand for growth, freedom, and transformation. Otherwise, I am void of integrity.

I allow only those people I know, like, and trust and who bring positive and joyful energy into my space, my circle of trust.

I have a zero-tolerance policy towards physical and emotional bullying, control and manipulation.

I do not associate myself with narcissistic behaviour, liars, cheats, or anyone who disrespects me, judges me, or criticises me or my loved ones in any way.

I speak to others how I would like to be spoken to (respectfully and lovingly).

I do not consume alcohol, smoke cigarettes, vapes, or take any mood-altering drugs to have a good time.

I am responsible for my well-being. This includes eating sufficient, nutritious food, drinking plenty of water, getting sufficient sleep and exercise, and having a balanced lifestyle.

I work only with companies, and clients who I align with, who I feel in complete integrity with, and who are a good fit for my career development.

I do not do business with any company that has previously terminated my work contracts. I have a zero-tolerance policy on this.

If it's to be, it's up to me. I take full responsibility for my actions and resulting consequences.

I am committed to everything I start, as I believe 100% is possible, 100% of the time.

I am living my life on my terms, where I am in complete control of my vision and my destiny.

I am living my life as if my life and other people's lives depend on it. We only get one shot at life…I am living my life the way I choose.

I am committed to being the best version of me… as giving and generous as I can possibly be.

I live a judgement-free and critical-free lifestyle. I offer personal and professional support, guidance, and coaching to the best of my ability, offering neutral feedback.

I am committed to empowering and inspiring other people to believe in themselves and to enrol in their own vision.

I believe in equality, and I do not discriminate against anyone. We are all equal and I have the utmost love and respect for all human beings.

I am committed to having a real deep connection with people whether we meet in person (face-to-face) or virtually and I shall show empathy and compassion towards their story.

What is my participation in life?

Our lives are very precious, and we are empowered to make the most out of them. We have the capacity to shape our experiences, create meaningful relationships, and live with purpose and clarity. However, in order to do this effectively, it is essential for us to understand how we are participating in life and the ways in which our individual contributions can influence the outcomes around us. In other words, the impact we have on the world.

Participation in life is a delicate balance between understanding how to take a step back and observe life from an objective perspective, as well as knowing when to confidently move forward with positive action. When this balance is maintained, we can experience growth in every area of our life. To effectively participate in life means that we must be aware of our power when it comes to decisions made surrounding our lifestyle choices. This awareness allows us to make informed decisions, which will ultimately shape our lives as a whole.

One of the most important steps towards gaining clarity on our participation in life is self-reflection. Taking time each day or week to sit down and assess where we're at, how we're feeling, and what progress has been made can be extremely beneficial for our growth process. Not only can this help us stay aligned with our goals, but it can also keep us accountable for our actions. Another great tool for gaining insight into our participation in life is meditation or mindfulness practices, such as yoga or walking. These activities allow us to be present in the moment without judgement or expectation, thus allowing ourselves time to process our thoughts more clearly while creating a deeper connection with ourselves.

Exposing ourselves regularly to new experiences can have such a positive effect…whether it be through travel or becoming involved with an organisation or community that resonates with our values. Being open to exploring beyond what feels comfortable, pushes us out of our comfort zones and also challenges us to grow, both mentally and spiritually.

Overall, participation in life is about engaging fully; it's about having faith that what we do matters, while courageously going after whatever sets our soul on fire. It's about listening closely for guidance from within, so that we may make decisions that bring fulfilment, rather than disappointment. It's about recognising the path ahead may not always be clear, but having confidence that no matter where it leads, there will always be something valuable gained along the way if we remain true to ourselves along every step of the journey.

"How are you participating in life? How are you showing up in life?"

What I learned from this leadership program was that I have been playing way too small a role in life. Through participating in this leadership program, I was able to recognise the importance of stepping out of my comfort zone and taking on bigger challenges, pushing myself to be the best version of myself.

Up until now, I have limited my life so much, have been playing the victim of so many rejections, that I could not see what was possible. I now have the awareness to remove these limiting four walls that I have trapped myself in, to now create a limitless life of endless possibilities. I have always been a go-getter, but I was amazed at how much further I could reach when I allowed myself to think bigger and take on larger goals than what I normally would. If I feel stretched, then I'm growing.

One of the most important lessons from the program was that it is essential to keep striving for more and to never be content with just settling into a routine… following everyone else, chasing their dreams. We were reminded throughout this intensive program that when we push ourselves to our limits, we can achieve great things. We can achieve our vision.

All in all, this leadership program opened my eyes to a world of possibilities beyond what I thought was achievable before participating in it. By focusing on a different perspective on life, having a positive attitude, and developing a growth mindset instead of staying within my own limitations, I was able to gain an invaluable amount of knowledge that will help me continue striving towards greater heights throughout my life. It has given me the belief and confidence that I get to become my most powerful, authentic, and loving self, where I can transform not only my life but the lives of millions of people around the world.

Can we really ever trust anyone?

When it comes to trust, I discovered that I naturally trust people by default. I give people an opportunity to show their true self, without judgement. I need to get to know someone before I have any doubts about them. To make my assessment of them, I would understand their character, their behaviour, their body language, their smile, their attitude, their energy, the words they use, and their feelings towards me, for example, are they loving, caring, supporting, empathetic or are they selfish, inconsiderate, hurtful? Are they consistent in what they say? Do they contradict themselves all the time?

Here is my definition of trust...

"Having confidence, faith in a person, being content and relaxed with someone, knowing they will never let you down, always there to support you, guide you when you're lost. They have no intention of hurting you or your family. They will protect you, no matter what. They have your back and they never go against their word to betray you. You believe everything they say and do."

To me, trust runs parallel to love, and respect. These are the three foundational pillars of a healthy relationship. This applies to family, work colleagues, an intimate relationship, basically anybody you meet. Without these three pillars, a solid relationship does not exist.

Trust is not something that can be built overnight, but instead requires dedication and commitment from both parties involved. To build trust, communication needs to be clear and consistent. Both people must be open and honest with each other about their thoughts and feelings, to create an environment of mutual respect and understanding. Additionally, it is important to remember that trust does not always mean blindly believing what the other person says; it means being able to rely on them, even when things are uncertain or difficult.

It is also important for those involved in a relationship to demonstrate shared values. This could involve pursuing similar interests together, discussing common life goals, or making joint decisions about major life changes, such as getting married or starting a family. Doing so helps both individuals feel more connected with one another.

In addition to communication and shared values, it is essential to show genuine care and concern for one another's well-being; both physically and emotionally. This involves checking up on each other's mental health regularly, as well as providing comfort when needed. It also includes providing support during times of difficulty or distress, which can help build strength within the bond between two people who share a trusting relationship, or friendship. Trust is earned over time through actions, rather than words alone. It takes patience and effort from both individuals involved in order for a trusting partnership to exist.

From my many traumatic rejection experiences and from the power of this leadership program, I have learned many things relating to trust, which include:

Find a global community, a safe space of like-minded people who you know will not judge or criticise you, and who will support you through your journey of life. For me, these people are entrepreneurs... truly inspiring and empowering leaders.

Never go into a relationship without having set strict boundaries. These are your ground rules that ensure you are transparent about what you want, but most importantly, this ensures you are protected from being hurt.

Always be alert for the red flags. Watch out for any signs of manipulation. Again, this is so you are protecting yourself from more pain and suffering.

Listen to what people say and observe to see if what they're saying aligns with their actions. A disconnect, contradiction, and inconsistency here is a really big warning sign to me.

Listen to the advice your family and close friends give to you. They know you better than anyone, probably more than you know yourself.

Remove people from your life who no longer serve you. This is if they lie, cheat, manipulate, and bully you or others in any way (emotionally or physically). These people have no right to be in your circle of friends.

Reskill, invest in yourself, and invest in personal development and business development programs. Commit 100% and trust the process so you can be self-sufficient and self-reliant. If you don't trust it, then it's not for you.

Trust yourself and believe in your own power and ability. Trust that you CAN live the life you want…it's your vision.

"Would you go into a marriage with someone you don't trust?"
"Would you work for a company you don't trust?"
"Without trust, there is no relationship" - Fran Wilson

Have I been playing it safe in my life?

Up until this point, I believe I have been playing it safe in my life…For so many years, I have been hiding behind four walls that kept me trapped in with my limiting beliefs, self-doubt, and nerds (those voices in my head). These are what kept telling me that I'm not good enough. This has suffocated me from living my best life, and it's known as living in my comfort zone. This comfort zone is where most people live, me included, for most of their lives. However, if I'm honest, I believe this to be the worst place to live. In fact, I believe this to be the source of self-sabotage.

"Our comfort zone is where we stop growing." - Fran Wilson

Living in our comfort zone is an easy, safe place to stay put. It can also be a way of robbing ourselves of a fulfilled life. My journey towards leaving my comfort zone began with acknowledging that I had been playing it safe for far too long and I needed to make changes in order to move forward.

So firstly, I took steps to identify my limiting beliefs and how they were holding me back. Some of these were what society had taught me in that I was only average, and not extraordinary. I was to follow everyone else, by going to college and university, gaining a degree, and then getting a job in the corporate world. I would just fit in. Other limiting beliefs revolved around the fear of making mistakes or being judged by others if I tried something new.

I then worked hard to challenge these thoughts and replace them with more positive ones, and what I had learned in this leadership program in managing my nerds, feeding them when they needed quieting down. This helped me to start seeing opportunities and possibilities, rather than obstacles, and gave me the courage to take risks. It was important during this time to remember that failure is part of growth and learning. So rather than seeing each rejection as defeat, I was able to embrace it as part of my journey towards success. Although this wasn't easy, I had to manage my emotions and thoughts, and the only way to do this was a mindset shift. That is, moving from a fixed and victim mindset to a growth mindset, with limitless possibilities.

Next, I started setting goals around how I wanted to live my life - from career aspirations to personal development goals, such as building healthy relationships, or mastering a new skill. With each goal achieved, no matter how small or big, came a sense of accomplishment, which motivated me further on my mission out of my comfort zone.

These goals included:

A four-month intensive transformational leadership program. This completely changed my perspective on how I saw myself and others. Write and publish this book to inspire others on how to overcome a lifetime of rejection and abandonment. I want to raise awareness that it's okay to not be okay, and that people are not alone.

Build a **Life Transformation Academy** where I passionately get to support, guide, and coach people all around the world in becoming rejection-proof, breaking free from all of this fear and pain of rejection and abandonment, so that they can live the life they dream of…they get to live their joyful vision with growth, freedom, transformation, belief, and confidence.

Gain clarity and define my new personal boundaries and raise my own standards in life.

Build a new circle of friends, where we all love, trust and respect one another.

Be kind to myself and reward myself with things I'm passionate about.

This is done by shifting to a powerful growth mindset, with my new mantra, *"Oh what the F*ck, go for it anyway"*, and stop getting in my way. For me, rewarding myself is things like booking a motorsport weekend to watch some racing and have some fun.

Mastering digital marketing skills, so that I can share my story and my rejection experiences with the world. I have invested a significant amount of time, money, and energy in digital marketing skills, such as learning how to run YouTube video ads, setting up Google Ad campaigns, sales funnels, email marketing and so much more.

Master the art of **diversification**…Not relying on one source of income to financially protect myself and my family. I believe in building a financial portfolio, where money works for you, and you can live your life joyfully, knowing you have built up multiple streams of income, whilst not relying solely on the traditional system, trading your time for money.

All of these goals took me out of my comfort zone. I was doing things I had never done before. These were stretching me to my limit. Some more than others. However, these stretches were necessary for me to become the person I was born to be.

I have come to realise that there are different zones in human psychology, and whatever mindset you're in will influence your zone.

The Comfort Zone is the place where most of us live, and for good reason. It allows us to feel safe, protected and secure in our environment, knowing that we are unlikely to encounter any surprises or challenges. For many of us, it's also a place of 'comfort' – somewhere we can go and relax without having to worry about what might happen. However, while this is a great way to keep ourselves protected from harm, it's also a hindrance if we want to grow as individuals.

Personally, I believe this way of living limits our potential. This is because the Comfort Zone prevents us from learning new things and pushing ourselves. As such, it's important that we find ways to break free from this fixed mindset, so that we can make progress and reach our fullest potential. To do this, we must move into different zones within our psychology – such as the Fear Zone, Learning Zone, and Growth Zone.

The Fear Zone, where most of us tend to go when faced with something unfamiliar or challenging. This is where our instincts kick in and make us feel scared or anxious – causing us to shy away from anything that could possibly cause harm or danger. While an element of fear can protect us from dangerous situations, an excessive amount can hold us back in life, as it prevents us from taking risks or trying something new. In order to overcome this fear-based mindset and push us in a more positive direction, we need courage, bravery, commitment and determination.

After the fear phase, we have the Learning Zone, which is one of the best places for personal growth and development – especially given how much knowledge there is available these days through digital technology. Here we can learn about anything under the sun – from business skills to self-improvement techniques – all while having fun along the way! This type of on-demand eLearning helps cultivate a mindset that encourages growth, rather than stagnation and procrastination; allowing us to develop skills that will serve us well later on down the line.

Finally, there is the Growth Zone, which is arguably one of the most important zones in terms of personal development. Here, people are able to turn ideas into reality by putting them into action, which enables them to become more confident in their abilities over time and eventually realise their potential. The key here is that growth doesn't happen overnight; you have to be persistent and consistent in your efforts if you want tangible results over time. You have to be 100% committed and follow through with what you set out to achieve.

The world is rapidly changing, and it has become increasingly important for everyone to stay up to date with the latest trends and developments in their respective fields. Therefore, to remain competitive and relevant in the modern world we live in, adaptability and flexibility are vital skills for any individual or organisation. Without them, stagnation can occur, leading to an inability to keep up with advancing technology and modern ways.

It is essential that all individuals remain aware of their surroundings, and constantly strive to better themselves through self-improvement. This means learning new skills, whether at a formal institution or through self-taught methods such as on-demand eLearning courses or coaching programs. When combined with hard work and dedication, these skills can bring about immense benefits, ranging from increased career prospects to improved financial status or financial freedom.

However, it is important to note that adapting and pivoting can be challenging at times, especially when changes occur faster than we are prepared for, or do not result in desirable outcomes - for example, all of my job losses. It can be especially difficult for those who have been accustomed to comfortable routines that no longer align with present conditions. Despite this challenge, the potential rewards far outweigh the risks involved in taking such steps toward improvement.

In today's ever-changing cost-of-living environment, where jobs and resources are becoming increasingly scarce, being able to make quick decisions and pivot on the fly is essential for survival. Knowing how to take calculated risks to stay ahead of the competition is a valuable skill that will serve you well throughout your life, but it's a skill that is only acquired through experience and practice.

Therefore, it is critical for any individual or business owner who wishes to remain successful over time, no matter what industry they operate in or what challenges they may face, to understand the importance of staying relevant by constantly adapting their approaches as needed, so they not just survive in this ever changing world, but thrive.

"I choose to…"

When I enrolled in this leadership program, I came to realise that my life was about to change. Although it was a bit intimidating at first, I decided to trust the process and make the most of it. Little did I know that the biggest lesson I would learn had nothing to do with the program itself, but with my own way of thinking.

This program quickly taught me how our thoughts had an effect on our life experiences. Here is an example of how that might look. Instead of saying, "I have to go to work today", we should say, "I choose to go to work today". This simple change of mindset could create a drastic change in our mental attitude in all aspects of our lives.

At first, this concept seemed strange and uncomfortable for me - how could such a small change make such a big difference? But, since I wanted to make the most out of the program, I decided to give it a try. I had to approach this with an open mind.

As time went by, my perspective completely changed! Instead of forcing myself to complete activities that were part of my everyday routine or tasks that required more effort than usual, by saying "I choose to" before engaging in them, everything became easier and more enjoyable.

It felt like I suddenly had control over all aspects of my life again; from going through mundane daily activities with renewed enthusiasm, taking care of myself better, and making healthier decisions for myself...this one tiny shift in mindset completely transformed my experiences in life!

This new way of looking at things turned out to be very powerful indeed; not only because it made tasks easier and less overwhelming, but also because it reminded me that every choice I make is ultimately up to me and no one else can decide for me. So now when something needs doing or if there is something important happening in my life, instead of feeling like, "I have to do this," or "this has been imposed upon me," I remember that in reality, "I choose to do this," and therefore regain control over my situation. Here are just a few things in life I choose to be, do, and have.

I choose to be happy
I choose to be free
I choose to be the best version of myself

I choose to be kind to myself

I choose to be the best dad for my children, Faye and Sara

I choose to be there for my loved ones whenever they need my support

I choose to be free from judging other people.

I choose to be accepting of judgement and criticism

I choose to be a powerful leader and coach

I choose to be my authentic self

I choose to be loving

I choose to be caring, considerate, kind, empathetic

I choose to be brave and courageous

I choose to be present

I choose to be honest, open, and transparent

I choose to be within integrity with my core values

I choose to be aligned with my vision

I choose to be self-sufficient and self-reliant

I choose to be vulnerable, and open-minded

I choose to be in control of my destiny

I choose to be willing to learn new skills

I choose to be financially free by building a financial portfolio

I choose to stand for growth, freedom, and transformation

I choose to live my healthiest life on my terms

I choose to do my best in life and show up powerfully for others

I choose to do what's best for me and my loved ones

I choose to do the right things in life with good intentions

I choose to feel great

I choose to be unstoppable

I choose to play the biggest game in life and win

I choose to be relentless

I choose to be responsible

I choose to be resilient

I choose to break free from toxic and negative environments

I choose to give myself permission to live my life how I want

I choose to work hard and reward myself accordingly

I choose to engineer and validate my own life on my terms

I choose to be a major contribution to changing the world for the better

I choose to overcome rejection by facing it head-on and being rejection-proof.

What do you "choose" in your life? Who do you "choose" to be?

Can you hear those rackets and nerds?

Rackets are ways in which we avoid something. We all have different flavours of rackets. Your racket runs continuously because again, you are trying to protect something or avoid it. Ask yourself, does your racket make you want to fight or hide? Do you freeze or fawn?

Here are some examples of our rackets…

Pain, fear, guilt, victim, anger, worry, martyr, anxiety, sadness, sickness, suffering, pity, tiredness, jealousy, boredom, depression, resentment, feeling raw, embarrassment, humiliation, worthlessness, disappointment, overwhelm.

Nerds are ways of being that lead to our actions. Rackets are an action step that doesn't work within our nerd. We run rackets instead of being in our contract (who we are) and taking action steps toward our vision. Your racket is the record player of things you've been telling yourself your whole life. Your nerd just pops up when something has been triggered.

I think we can all relate to these rackets and nerds. These just seem to be a part of our lives. But it's now having that awareness and recognising when they dictate the trajectory of our lives. The leadership program taught me strategies on how to manage, control, and overcome these rackets and nerds. This is what motivated me to write this book in the first place.

What are the prices you pay?

When faced with our nerds, those voices in our heads telling us we can't do something, it's important to recognise them for what they are: simply thoughts that can be changed if we choose differently. For example, if the thought is, "I'm not smart enough" then we can counter that with, "I am capable and have everything within me necessary to achieve success." Ultimately, facing our fears head-on will enable us to live an extraordinary life outside the confines of our comfort zone.

This shift in mindset is critical in managing these nerds or voices in my head. That's why I get to take back control of those rejection and abandonment voices…telling me that I'm not good enough, not good enough to be in a healthy loving relationship, or in a secure engineering job that I'm passionate about. Well I am good enough. And so are you.

One of the biggest blocks to actually being responsible is your resistance to feeling bad. Shame and guilt are powerful emotions that most people don't want to feel (or feel more of). Rather than feeling guilt or shame, it is much easier to be a victim to the circumstance occurring, or possibly to blame someone or something else as to why that event happened. The negative feelings of being a victim have an underlying motivation or payoff.

Payoffs come from 'The Blame Game' we play in life. The negative feelings of being a victim or feeling victimised are called 'grungies'. Your 'grungies', however, have an underlying motivation or payoff.

1 - RECOGNITION: Approval, Recognition, Sympathy, Validation, Attention (positive or negative). When you are acting like a victim, you often have people feeling sorry for you, validating your experience, or giving you attention.

Antidote: Ask for what you want. For example: "I would like to be acknowledged for how hard I am working on this project, even though it is not finished yet."

2 - DECEPTION OF OTHERS: Control, Manipulation, Domination. Sometimes in being a victim, you control the energy of the room or the conversation. You dominate the moment with your victim story or upset.

Antidote: Be honest/vulnerable. For example: "I am feeling hurt right now in this conversation. Could you say that another way?"

3 - PROTECTION: Being right. This one is a bit tricky. You may be right about your limiting beliefs or lack of value. "Look how hard I try, and nothing turns out."

Antidote: Let go. Take a risk and be courageous. For example: "I want to be right that I am not the best choice for that new position; however, I am going to be brave and go for it."

4 - EXCUSE FOR: Circumstances, external forces, and conditions have power over you. You feel like you are powerless in the face of the conditions around you, and you can use that as your story or excuse not to succeed.

Antidote: Own it, choose responsibility, and believe in your power to make it happen. For example: "It seems like the conditions are challenging, but I must be up to the challenge, and I believe I can do it!"

"What is the payoff you get out of running that racket (approval, control, playing it safe, being right, victim, overwhelm, attention, sympathy, procrastinating, avoiding responsibility, manipulation of others, superior, protecting your image of yourself)?"

"What are the prices others pay for your rackets? Is it safety and security, empathy, trust, belief, approval, compassion?"

Personally, from this initial phase of the program "Vision", I learned that I'm no longer hiding behind excuses, stories or my fears. This was a real wake-up call for me. I experienced a flashback of my entire life, such as my career, teenage years, childhood, and my love life.

Betrayal and broken agreements have impacted my life and have prevented me from being the person I was born to be. They have caused so much anger, hurt and depression, which over time, has made me feel trapped. I lost trust in so many areas of my life. The price I've already paid is not having better relationships (family, partners). Not being the dad my girls need. Being unhappy, lacking confidence and belief in myself. I have become the victim of my own story.

When I remove my armour of rackets and payoffs, many new possibilities open up for me;

I get to give myself permission to be me
I get to give myself the love that I deserve (self-love)
I get to trust myself and the process of life
I get to feel worthy
I get to believe in myself and my ability
I get to manage and control my nerds, so they don't control me
I get to break through my limiting beliefs to create a limitless lifestyle

I get to transition from a "fixed mindset" to a "growth mindset"

I get to be powerful

I get to be my true authentic self

I get to be loving

I get to grow…if I'm not growing, I'm dying

I get to be free

I get to be open, honest, and transparent about anything in life

I get to transform the lives of millions of people around the world

I get to be present, in the moment, and live in the now

I get to let go of all this heavy baggage that has been weighing me down

I get to rewrite my story, my way, on my terms

I get to be in charge of my life and my destiny

I get to be the best proud dad for my children

I get to create financial freedom with my thriving and successful businesses

I get to express my voice because my voice matters

I get to express my feelings and opinions without the fear of judgement

I get to create new friendships

I get to invest in me

I get to create new business Joint-Venture (JV) partnerships

I get to be in a happy, healthy, loving intimate relationship with a partner who loves me for who I am

I get to share my vision, my purpose with the world

I get to have a positive impact on so many lives

I get to support, guide, and coach those who are passionate about living their vision

I get to offer my gift to the world and empower and inspire millions of people.

This is what's possible when I am committed to playing a bigger game in life, and show up for myself and other people in the way that I know I can. I also learned and acknowledged that I get to let go of so many things that are holding me back from living my best and highest version of me. It's not easy letting go of people I love, or a job I was so passionate about, but this is what must happen in order for me to move forward with my life…a new life of not being afraid of rejection and abandonment. And you can have the very same…a new life where you have overcome your fear of rejection.

In Breakthrough, I shattered everything that was not working for me. I redefined how I was showing up in the world and I discovered how to operate from a new place of possibility. I left the past firmly behind and I walked into my future as a powerful leader.

As I started this phase of the program, I noted in my journal how I was feeling and what was about to happen.

"I'm about to start phase 2 (Breakthrough) of my life transformation program HCL40. This is a four-part phase and again like vision, is very intensive. For me, the hours are 5pm until 5am. So I'm focused for 12 hours throughout the night for four nights. This is what I do to invest in myself. I want to be the absolute best version of myself. I do not accept being average anymore."

This was the moment when I had to declare a new vision. I know I just completed the vision phase of the program. However, that was setting the foundations so I could gain clarity and declare my new vision.

*"My vision is to __authentically__ create a world of
__Freedom,__ Connection, Peace, __Love__ and Abundance, where we all
take responsibility to unleash the __power__
and potential within us, so that we, as __leaders,__ can live
an unstoppable life of __growth,__ and __transformation."__
- Fran Wilson*

We need feedback to grow

Feedback is an essential part of any healthy relationship, both professional and personal. To ensure a successful relationship, it is important to provide feedback in a non-judgmental, constructive manner.

When providing feedback, the most important thing to remember is that your primary focus should be on the behaviour rather than the person. This means you can tell someone what they did wrong, without attacking them personally. For example, instead of saying, "You are so selfish" you could say, "I felt hurt when you didn't offer to help me with a task". This way you are expressing how their behaviour affected you, but are not attacking them as a person.

Another tip for providing effective feedback is to ensure that it is timely and specific. People often give general comments about their opinion or feelings without really telling the other person what they need to do differently. It can be helpful to provide examples of situations in which certain behaviours were not helpful so that the other person has clarity over the changes they can make in the future.

Finally, it is important to be open to receiving feedback from others as well. This is a two-way dialogue. A great way to start this process is by asking people for their input and listening attentively, without feeling overly defensive or sensitive when trying to make improvements in your relationships or at work. It also helps if you show appreciation and gratitude for people's suggestions and thank them for taking the time out of their day to provide valuable insight into your performance or situation.

One of the eye-opening experiences that I faced was when I received feedback from other members of the leadership program group (HCL40).

The feedback that hurt me the most...

CO-DEPENDENT - It was hard to hear this. I don't want to find my happiness and validation through other people, but somehow, I programmed myself to rely on others to feel safe and secure, such as in an intimate relationship. This was the moment I chose to break that cycle.

My experience of this feedback was that it was a very big wakeup call for me. It opened my eyes to what others see in me. It's hard to hear the truth, yet I accepted my feedback, positive and negative. This now applies at any time in my life. If it helps me to grow and unleash my potential and the power within, then I shall receive it with gratitude.

I'm not afraid anymore. Life is now, and it's time to stop hiding behind these masks of self-sabotage. It's time to stop playing the small game and to go all-in. I want to be independent. I want to be free and be my true authentic self. I accept the fact that the co-dependency no longer serves me. So I was committed to standing up and facing these demons and jumping over the line to independence.

Here are some questions I was asking myself:

What's missing in my relationships with other people?
Trust, love, appreciation, respect, acceptance, acknowledgement, inclusion, belief, compassion, affection.

What's missing in my relationship with myself?
Self-Love, self-respect, honesty, belief, confidence.

The masks/images that I project are?
People-pleasing, lack of self-love, sensitive, unworthy, lack of confidence, lack of leadership, lack of authority and control of my life, vulnerability.

The pain/hurt/suffering that I have been covering up?
Rejection and abandonment trauma, narcissistic bullying, unwanted feeling, unworthy, voiceless, lack of trust, lack of belief in my ability.

What I'm avoiding/resisting in my life?
Being kind to myself, looking after me instead of everyone else, going all-in, playing the biggest game in life, letting go of things and people that no longer serve me or add value to my life. Facing my demons and confronting my ego.

But first I had to confront a few people (in my own head) who have impacted my life...from a rejection and abandonment perspective. This was something that I had to do to release the demons, and also be at peace with each of these people and experiences. I spoke to my inner child, reassured him that I would protect him from now on. I put my inner child back into my heart, where it belonged.

To be clear, I have no resentment towards these people, I simply have just love, respect and acceptance for who they are. I needed to confront:

My biological father for abandoning me before I was even born.
My adopted father who abandoned me when I was 13 years old.
My first love, who left me when I was 21 years old.
The bullies in my secondary school.

My so-called best friend in the transmission rig test facility.
My team leader in the chassis engineering team.
The company that served me three job losses, treated me like just a number, and disrespected me.

The mother of my children for taking our girls under a police escort and walking out on me on Faye's seventh birthday.

The racing team that no longer wanted me in their team.

My partner of over five years who manipulated me, bullied and abused me, both mentally and emotionally. I expressed my anger, excruciating pain, hurt and suffering towards her for not believing in me, for her narcissistic bullying, and for walking out on me (when she said I was the ONE).

This was one of the hardest things I had ever done. However, in order to overcome my fear of rejection, I am now committed to creating an environment that encourages positive self-esteem and acceptance, where we all feel worthy and loved. To do this, I focus on building meaningful ten out of ten relationships with those around me. I concentrate on cultivating mutual respect and understanding, towards different opinions and points of view. Learning to appreciate other perspectives helps us become more tolerant of ourselves and others.

I am developing healthy coping mechanisms for dealing with the fear of rejection. This includes identifying negative thought patterns associated with fear and replacing them with positive affirmations ("I get to…", "I choose to…", "I am… "). This shall bring out the powerful voice within me, which will drown out the noise of these negative nerds and rackets. Additionally, I am setting realistic expectations for myself, rather than unattainable goals. I am learning how to be kind to myself and to celebrate small victories…small wins help me stay motivated, even when I experience rejection or failure.

Finally, I am dedicated to accepting responsibility for my actions, instead of placing blame on others or external circumstances…I am not playing the victim game any longer. Taking ownership of our choices allows us to learn from our mistakes and acquire new skills that can help us become a more confident leader in the future.

By taking these steps, I am hopeful that I am building a stronger sense of self-worth and a healthier attitude towards rejection and failure. With time, practice and patience, I know that it is possible to create a fulfilling life, despite having experienced rejection in the past. I am a powerful, authentic, loving leader and I stand for growth, freedom, and transformation. I am worthy…You are worthy…We are all worthy.

As the breakthrough phase progressed, I received more and more feedback from my teammates. They were open, honest, and transparent about what they saw in me. They provided me with their neutral feedback with so much love. Here are some of the feedback I received, with gratitude:

Scared little boy
Abandonment
Rejection
Loneliness
Victim
Stuck in my stories
Sadness.

Breakthrough is what guided me to defining my "I am" contract statement. This is the key to my power and it's who I truly am.

"I AM A POWERFUL, AUTHENTIC, LOVING LEADER" -
Fran Wilson

What are you committed to creating?

I also discovered that I have been completely disconnected from areas of my life, especially in my career and intimate relationships.

With regards to my career, I never felt in control or in charge of how long each job would last. I was made redundant, and had my contract terminated at least six times in the space of seventeen years. These were not my decisions, but the HR and hiring manager in these large global brands that I worked in.

It was also very clear in my relationships. Up until this point, I had what I would consider three long-term relationships, where my partner left me in all three. I somehow had a big disconnect with each of them that affected our compatibility. These rejections created so many rackets in my head and made me question if I was good enough for anyone.

"Why did she leave me? What was it that I did wrong? Could I have done more? I don't understand"…

I constantly had that conversation with my ego, who always seemed to dominate. These voices got louder and louder. But to be honest, I will never understand, and I have to accept that.

This program changed the game for me. I felt like I was part of a loving, supporting and caring team.

Together, we got the opportunity to create a team vision statement that unified our team in a common vision. It was to be written in excellence as "We HCL40 are committed to creating a world of _ _ _ _, _ _ _ _, _ _ _ _, (3 to 5 words that represent our world vision). Here is what we discovered about ourselves and the world we want to live in…

"We HCL40 are committed to creating a world of Freedom, Peace, Connection, Love and Abundance"

As you can see, my own personal vision is completely aligned with our team vision. Life is an enrollment game and I am enrolled in my vision to create the life that I truly want and deserve. I am a transformational leader. The feedback I was getting from my teammates was now very different from before.

Courage
Confidence
Passion
Love
Freedom
Strength
Success in Abundance
Forgiveness
Gratitude
Broken-down walls
Tenacity
Grit
Happiness
Determined
Pushes against all odds
Go-Getter
Defies Exhaustion

Bad Ass.

Now, it's time to provide my feedback and experience of this leadership program.

It was powerful
It was life-changing
It was impactful
It was intense
It was challenging
It was an eye-opener and an awakening experience
It stretched me beyond belief
It took me out of my comfort zone, and through my fears towards my vision
It gave me so many breakthroughs
It helped me define who I am…my authentic self
It unleashed the leader inside of me
It gave me new standards and ground rules in life
It gave me clarity on my vision
It gave me new tools to work on my personal development, mindset, relationships, etc
It gave me my "Contract"
It gave me my voice back
It gave me my confidence back
It gave me hope and belief I'm capable of achieving my goals
It gave me new lifetime friends, "buddies" and connections
It made me feel loved, valued, and appreciated with no judgement
It gave me so many possibilities and opportunities in life
It made me feel unstoppable
It made me feel limitless and powerful
It made me feel worthy…I am worthy.

I want to ask you one question…What are you committed to creating?

What this leadership program taught me

Leadership means standing up not only for oneself, but also for others who cannot do the same for themselves. In doing so, we take responsibility to create a better world for everyone we interact with. We accept that we can make an impact no matter how small; we understand our power as individuals and unite in solidarity to fight injustice wherever it arises. Leadership is never passive; instead, it requires courage and action at every turn.

When we commit to being responsible leaders who stand for our beliefs, we become empowered to create real change in the world around us. We become agents of growth and transformation. With this newfound clarity on my personal mission statement comes increased confidence and self-awareness within myself, which allows me to approach any situation with strength and positivity while always staying true to my own inner truths.

Leadership gives us the ability to truly take responsibility for our part in creating the world we want to see around us: one full of growth, freedom, and transformation…a transformed world where everyone can feel safe, accepted, respected, heard and valued equally regardless of their race, gender or social background. As responsible leaders, we must continue striving towards this goal until all are free from injustice of any kind whatsoever.

The opposite of responsibility is victimhood. When we succumb to victimhood, we give away our personal power and surrender to our circumstances, without taking action to make things better. By rejecting this victim mindset and instead, taking ownership of our lives and the direction of our future, we create a powerful momentum towards achieving our goals and living a meaningful life. Here are the five leadership distinctions:

If it's to be, it's up to me (Responsibility).
100% is possible, 100% of the time (Commitment).
Live my life as if my life and other people's lives depended on it (Urgency).
Giving and Generosity (Service).
Committed action versus psychological assessment, where psychological assessment is my nerds, fears, judgements, and insecurities (Intentional Focus).

What's your personality style?

Our personality style, also known as social style can be thought of as an operating system that determines how we interact with our environment and the people around us. Knowing our own style of personality, as well as understanding the different styles of those close to us, can help us to better relate to others, understand differences in communication and problem-solving, and identify potential areas of miscommunication or conflict.

The four main personality styles are Controller (Driver), Promoter (Socialiser), Supporter (Relator) and Analyser (Thinker). People tend to have a primary style that is more dominant for them than any other. Depending on your environment and people you interact with, this style can flex or shift.

The Controller is task-oriented, highly structured and self-confident. They are often extroverted, assertive people who seek to direct the course of events. They prefer a logical approach to problem-solving and take charge of situations. They think quickly on their feet, are often decisive leaders, and enjoy taking risks.

The Promoter is outgoing, talkative, and sociable. They are more focused on interaction with other people, often attempting to build consensus among diverse groups or individuals. They are highly social in nature and enjoy being the life of the party. They often perform best in large groups, where they can network with people easily. They are highly driven by emotions and thrive when working collaboratively to bring ideas into fruition.

The Supporter is warm-hearted, loyal and values relationships deeply. They are focused on relationships and connecting with people emotionally, in order to create a sense of stability within their environment. They like having good quality conversations with friends and family members, in which they can get to know each other better. They prefer a supportive approach when problem-solving, rather than making quick decisions without considering feelings involved.

Finally, the Analyser is analytical, yet objective in their thinking process. They think through everything thoroughly before coming up with solutions or drawing conclusions about something. Often seen as quiet observers who like researching topics before stating opinions about them, they enjoy sharing knowledge with others, in order to expand their understanding of the world around them. They often take calculated risks when making decisions based on what they have seen or heard from others over time.

No matter what our primary style may be, it's important that we learn to recognise how our own personality style might differ from someone else's. Also, how it can be adapted in order to communicate better with those around us, so we can all create a harmonious relationship between ourselves, as well as those close to us.

As an individual, you may encompass some aspects of each personality style, but likely lean towards one particular type more than the others. For instance, I am classified as a Supporting Analyser…meaning that I possess both qualities of a Supporter and an Analyser, without leaning too heavily towards either side. This combination gives me the ability to both empathise with people, while also analysing situations in detail to make sound decisions.

It's important to recognise your primary personality style so you can better understand yourself, but also appreciate how other types work alongside yours in order to achieve greater success in whatever goals you are striving for. Learning about how your unique blend of traits interact with others, can help you identify areas for improvement within yourself while also enabling you to assess potential collaborators or employers. By uncovering your personality style flex, it will allow you greater insight into why certain situations turn out differently than expected, as well as how best to approach new tasks or challenges that come your way throughout life's journey.

What was missing in my leadership?

At the core of successful leadership is the ability to take charge and motivate others. It is a complex mix of various qualities, which sadly, I had been lacking. A few of these qualities included confidence, commitment, power, discipline, authority, courage, bravery, generosity, compassion, empathy, going above and beyond expectations, passion and desire to achieve goals, motivation, belief in myself, self-love and self-trust. This is an area of my life that I'm focused on and will continue to develop.

What was not working in my ways of being and attitude?

Some of my ways of being and attitude were not working either. These included not being authentic or sticking to my word, demonstrating a lack of integrity with my contracts (both verbal and written), failing to instil trust in others; showing a lack of credibility or responsibility, and not being present or committed to the task at hand. Again this is an area that I'm fully committed to. Being my authentic self with a positive attitude is what shall take me on the right path to growing into the person I was born to be. There is zero-tolerance for complacency or deviating from this.

What limiting beliefs showed up in my life the most?

My limiting beliefs or 'rackets' that were constantly presenting themselves in my life were that I was constantly playing the victim role, feeling overwhelmed by many things in life, having a perfectionist attitude that hindered progress instead of helping it along the way, over analysing situations (being the analyser I am!), which led to inaction rather than action…and finally, feeling unworthy and lacking in confidence when faced with challenging moments, such as losing so many jobs and relationships.

These combined issues led me on a journey towards understanding what I needed to do differently, in order for me to become a better leader. To start this process, I did some deep reflection on where I was going wrong - both within myself, as well as with how I interacted with others - so that I could identify areas for improvement. This was how I invested in myself, by enrolling in leadership programs, like the one I've mentioned. I'm always investing my time, money, and commitment into other personal and business development communities and academies. This is so that I can gain the confidence, education and knowledge to live my life on my terms, by being self-reliant, self-sufficient and in complete control of my own destiny.

Using practical tools such as mindset shift strategies, goal setting, and meditation techniques that allowed me to tap into higher levels of consciousness, I was able to begin making positive changes within myself. Slowly, these then translated into improved interactions externally. As a result, my leadership abilities began improving through increased self-awareness, more belief and confidence in myself, which has then continued over time due to the continual learning process that comes with growth through experience.

Where did these nerds come from?

It can be difficult enough to navigate the everyday stresses of life. But when a person experiences a relationship failure, job loss, or financial stress, just like I did, the emotional toll can be magnified significantly. It affects individuals on all levels... physically, mentally, spiritually and emotionally.

Relationship failures - These can bring up feelings of hurt, betrayal, guilt, anger, fear and shame. A breakup can cause us to doubt our ability to make meaningful connections in the future and leave us feeling isolated and afraid. I know too well what this feels like. But, you have to go through the pain, and come out the other side with more strength, to overcome this fear of rejection.

Job losses - Losing one job, or experiencing one contract termination is a very traumatic and stressful time. However, losing at least six jobs, like I did, is hard to put into words. I will never understand how it happened or why it happened, but it did. However, it's how we respond and deal with it is a real test of who we are. Even to this day, I know what it feels like to be rejected from a company (multiple times)…it brought up feelings of worthlessness, being unwanted or a surplus to requirement. I could go on. This lack of control is a difficult thing to accept without feeling helpless. But again, you have to go through the pain, face your fears head on, and come out the other side with more strength and more determination to overcome this fear of rejection.

Judgement and criticism - Being judged or criticised by others can also have a deep emotional effect, due to our need for connection in relationships. Criticism makes us feel misunderstood by those closest to us, which leads to feelings of loneliness even while surrounded by people who love us. For me, this constant criticism from loved ones was really tough to take. But again, if we allow the right people into our trusted circle of friends, this can be overcome.

Financial stress and anxiety - With my constant search for new employment, after each job loss, I was always filled with financial stress and anxiety. I had been searching for new employment for what felt like an eternity. The searches usually lasted three to six months at a time, and the stress and anxiety that came with this was overwhelming. It seemed to be never ending, affecting my mental and emotional health.

The uncertainty of it all created a storm of emotions that I battled daily. Additionally, the financial pressure was immense – I had to make ends meet in order to keep up with my living expenses, while also trying to save for future endeavours.

My search meant countless hours spent on job sites and networking events trying to find something suitable, yet nothing ever worked out. There were times when my job applications would go unanswered or worse yet – when I got the dreaded rejection email in response to my hard work and effort. This motivated me to continue pushing forward, but at the same time caused a great deal of internal turmoil, which took its toll on me mentally and physically.

Not only did I feel disappointed when things didn't turn out how I had hoped, but the added financial pressure exacerbated these feelings. Without income from a consistent job, covering my household bills became increasingly difficult; however, I refused to give up hope, as it was my only lifeline in such dire circumstances….and I never quit.

The months went by without any luck in finding new employment, yet I remained resilient throughout it all, hoping that someday something would finally come through for me and offer some reprieve from my struggles. Despite the obstacles, there is always light at the end of every tunnel if you're willing to keep pushing forward and try your best, no matter what comes your way. But as I've learned and will always repeat, we cannot rely on one source of income.

Finally, it's easy to become overwhelmed by your emotions and struggles — but it's important to remember that this is normal, given the circumstances you might be facing. It doesn't make you weak or inferior, but rather it shows how strong you are for facing these challenges head-on, instead of running away from them. With the right kind of support from family and friends, or professional help if needed, it is possible for you to deal with relationship failures, job losses, judgement and criticism from others, to find peace within yourself again, despite your current difficulties.

Living a life of personal growth requires courage and dedication, as well as the willingness to confront and accept fears. It is not an easy feat, especially if we are surrounded by people who may not believe or support us in our endeavours. Despite any objections from the outside world, it is important for us all to strive towards our vision for the future and take ownership of our transformation process. We must stand for a changed world.

As such, it is important to acknowledge our own accomplishments during this journey of life. It signifies that despite any obstacles encountered along the way - whether external or internal - progress has been made towards achieving our goals. Acknowledging ourselves for being brave, courageous, committed and vulnerable, can provide much needed insight into how far we have come on this journey of personal growth.

The act of acknowledging ourselves can be incredibly empowering. It helps to remind us that we are capable of achieving our dreams and gives us the motivation to continue to push forward when times get tough. By recognising our successes, we gain belief in ourselves and become more confident in our abilities to face any challenge that comes our way. We recognise that though fear may arise at certain points, it will never dictate where we go or what we achieve in life.

We must not forget that part of living a life of personal growth, freedom, and transformation includes learning from past experiences and mistakes, so that we aren't deterred from reaching our desired destination…our vision. Every setback should be seen as an opportunity for growth - an invitation to learn something new that will bring us closer to achieving our vision for the future. Through moments of triumph as well as moments of defeat, it is always important to stay true to ourselves and remain committed to our mission, without giving up hope or succumbing to negativity, self-doubt or self-sabotage.

It is also important never to forget our "Why". The reason we began this new path on our journey in the first place and the motivating factors driving us. By assessing these questions regularly throughout our journey, we can remain focused on our goals while at the same time, appreciating where we have already come from thus far – committing ourselves fully once more with each step taken forward on this path towards personal growth and transformation. And we do this by supporting one another, holding each other high.

We rise as one.

Personally, I acknowledge myself for facing my fears of rejection, abandonment, criticism and investing in my own personal growth, showing up, stretching myself, being committed to transforming my life and living my vision, being vulnerable, being courageous and brave, and believing in myself, when others didn't see my potential and power.

100 of my personal achievements in life

Here are 100 things that I have achieved in my life so far. This is not everything or an exhaustive list, just a select few that I have accomplished in my first forty years. This was an exercise one of my business coaches gave me when I invested in leadership and business coaching (alongside HCL40 in the same community). It was a tough challenge for me to compile this list, but I completed it, and surprisingly I really enjoyed doing this. My target was to complete this within one hour. I managed to get to 100 in 57 minutes and 53 seconds.

I learned how to walk.
I learned how to speak English.
I learned how to ride a bicycle.
I learned how to tie my shoe laces.
I learned how to get dressed.
I learned how to write.
I learned how to read.
I learned how to make friends.
I learned how to climb trees.
I learned how to do cartwheels (gymnastics).
I learned how to play the recorder.
I learned how to make food.
I learned how to brush my teeth.
I learned how to use the toilet.
I learned how to roller skate.
I won player of the year in 1996 for my under 14s football team.
I smoked when I was 13, but quit after I suffered from bronchitis Christmas 1996. I have never smoked since then.
I overcame the hurt, pain, and suffering when my dad abandoned the family in 1996.
I played for many football teams.

I never got a yellow card in my 11-a-side football career.

I got my first job when I was 15 years old.

I got my first motorcycle (moped) when I was 16 years old.

I learned how to change the bed sheets.

I learned how to play decks as a DJ in my bedroom and record mixtapes.

I got my first girlfriend when I was 18 years old.

I moved away from home when I was 20 years old.

I got my first big motorcycle (600cc) in 2006.

I got a Diploma in Mechanical Engineering in Dublin in 2003.

I got a 2:1 in my Automotive degree in Oxford Brookes in 2005.

I got a Master's degree in Motorsport Vehicle Dynamics in 2006.

I got my first job in a global premium automotive company in 2006.

I rode a 125cc motorcycle across the UK and over to Ireland.

I rode a 600cc motorcycle across the UK and over to Ireland.

I got to test-drive luxury vehicles.

I qualified as an advanced driver in my automotive career (Level 5 Autonomous Driving).

I got to be one of a few people to drive a fully autonomous vehicle down the UK motorway.

I learned how to test transmission and driveline systems.

I learned how to measure vehicle ride comfort.

I learned how to develop Autonomous systems such as Adaptive Cruise Control.

I learned how to flash software and calibrations into vehicle control modules.

I learned how to test helicopter systems such as intermediate and tail gearboxes.

I commissioned and operated very complex rig tests.

I bought my first car in 2007.

I had my first child, Faye, in 2009 when I was 26 years old.

I had my second child, Sara in 2011.

I bought my first house in 2011 (a week before Sara was born).

I completed a 95-mile cycling sportif around the new forest and the Isle of Wight.

I overcame multiple job losses.

I shook the hand of Ratan Tata (Indian industrialist, philanthropist, and former chairman of Tata Sons, Chairperson of Jaguar Land Rover).

I had laser eye surgery.

I have been offered jobs at Bentley Motors and McLaren.

I have been offered a manager role in Saudi Arabia.

I sold my first family home in 2017.

I overcame a terrible relationship breakup with my children's mother.

I lost nearly 20 Kg in weight during the Covid pandemic.

I completed a 90-Day video journey.

I made my first sale online in 2020.

I've had 3 Covid Vaccinations.

I sold my second home in 2022.

I overcame being kicked out of my partner's house.

I learned how to build websites.

I learned how to set up YouTube Ad campaigns.

I learned how to set up sales funnels.

I learned how to create multiple streams of income and diversify.

I learned how to be recession-proof and self-reliant.

I learned how to create my own coaching program.

I learned how to get new clients in my business.

I have attended many business networking events and made great connections.

I learned how to create my own digital products.

I learned how to run a live virtual summit.

I learned how to run a pre-recorded virtual summit.

I learned how to set up an automated sales process.

I learned affiliate marketing.

I learned forex trading.

I invested in myself, my education.

I joined many entrepreneur communities around the world.

I have travelled to Dubai on Airbus A380 many times (my favourite aircraft).

I have worked on multi-million-pound hypercar projects.

I owned a £40k BMW.

I have done many motorcycle track days around the UK.

I have travelled to the Gold Coast, Australia on my own for personal and business development workshops.

I have travelled to Florida on my own for a mastermind event.

I drove a car in Florida and was very nervous (left-hand drive, other side of the road).

I invested in a transformational leadership program to achieve my highest potential.

I stayed up four nights in a row to attend practical workshops.

I quit drinking alcohol at the age of 39.

I have set new boundaries in life.

I have made health a high priority in my life.

I can live anywhere in the world.

I went from a 'fixed' mindset to a 'growth' mindset.

I discovered my contract. I am a powerful, authentic, loving leader.

I discovered what I stand for. I stand for growth, freedom, transformation.

I learned how to create a new personal brand and logo.

I learned how to broadcast zoom on Facebook Live.

I moved closer to my children in Dorset, UK.

I learned how to test and develop air-to-air flight refuelling systems and weapons carriers.

I have volunteered to help a brain charity and do fundraising for such a great cause.

I have the belief I can do anything.

I have given myself permission to challenge the status quo.

I learned how to develop flight controls software in helicopter cockpit simulators.

This was a really good exercise because it made me realise just how important I am in this world. It has made me reflect on all of the great things that I have achieved so far in my life, regardless of what obstacles I may have faced, such as multiple job losses, failed relationships and family abandonment. This has given me the space to feel a sense of pride, gratitude, and to really acknowledge just what I'm capable of.

So now, I want you to do the very same and list 100 things you have achieved in your life so far, so that you get to see your true greatness.

What is your superpower?

I was put on earth for a reason. There is a place for me, and I'm entitled to owning that place. I have a unique gift and I get to share that gift with the world. I believe in myself and what I'm capable of achieving in life.

I have many abilities, skills such as engineering, developing and validating pre-production systems, powerfully overcoming rejection, supporting and mentoring others to achieve their vision. Being a supporting analyser, I am always striving to find solutions to other people's problems.

I have the hunger, desire, passion, and commitment to succeed in life. I am very competitive and never like to lose. I always set the bar high for myself and I am very ambitious. So much so that it scares other people and at times, even myself. I will not quit. I have so much resilience and I am relentless in achieving my goals. I am loving, caring and always thinking of others before myself. I tend to people please, which I know is self-sabotaging. However, I am now focused on putting myself first. I have a kind, warm heart and nothing but 100% good intentions in life. I am loyal and trusting. I am kind and considerate. I do not take drugs (never have done), and I don't drink alcohol or smoke. I am a hard worker with a Master's degree in Motorsport Vehicle Dynamics. This was after I worked very hard to obtain a Bachelor's degree in Automotive Engineering. I am sensitive, compassionate, empathetic and I always listen to other people's problems. I have two gorgeous daughters, whom I get to protect. I love them with all my heart.

In an intimate relationship, I have the biggest heart. I give my partner whatever she wants and needs. I go the extra mile to make people happy. I am worthy of being here. I am a great person. I am a fighter and never give up. I am strong and powerful with so much love to give to the world. I mean no harm to anyone or anything. Whatever the world throws at me, I find a way to overcome the challenges, the pain, and look for a positive solution. I have a big vision to create a world of Freedom, Love, Peace, Connection, and Abundance. I was put on this earth to have a positive impact. I was born to transform the lives of millions of people.

I get to be Powerful, Authentic, and Loving.
I get to raise my standards and set new personal boundaries.
I get to be courageous and brave.
I get to be my authentic self.
I get to be the loving and supportive father my girls deserve.
I get to be the best father, brother, son, uncle, nephew, cousin, and friend I can be.
I get to be the most loving, affectionate partner that a woman deserves.
I get to give myself permission to be who I was born to be.
I get to gift myself with self-love, self-worth, and self-respect.

I get to be vulnerable.

I get to be bold.

I get to face my fear of rejection and abandonment.

I get to expand my box and break free from all of my limitations.

I get to be limitless and unstoppable.

I get to trust the process, the journey of life.

I get to be creative and design the life I want.

I get to remove these masks I've been wearing.

This is me…This is my superpower!

Who do you get to be?…What is your superpower?

What does empowerment even mean?

When I joined the 'Heartcore' Leadership community, I never truly knew who I was. I always thought I'd figure it out somehow, but it wasn't until this life-changing experience when I realised my true potential and who I'm meant to be. I mean, truly who I am and what exactly I stand for.

Powerful

When I say I'm powerful, I refer to having the right mindset, and having the desire and determination to keep going, to keep pushing forward no matter what comes my way. I have more resilience than I ever thought I had. I'm also relentless in pursuing my dreams. Nothing will ever stop me from reaching my goals and aspirations. I have the power to succeed and inspire others to reach their goals and vision.

Authentic

There is nothing more important than being authentic, and your true self. Everyone else is taken, so it's important to be yourself, and that's exactly what I'm doing. I'm being my pure self. I'm not trying to be something that I'm not. Authenticity is key to living a successful and honest life.

Loving

Where do I begin with this…Love is in my DNA. All I have is love in my body…love for myself and love for others. I do not know any other way of being except for love. I love everyone with all my heart and I will never stop loving. I love my children. I love my family and friends, and I hope and pray for a world of love and peace.

People that know me, know how much love I have for everyone. Every cell of my body is filled with love for others. My love for those around me is truly extraordinary. It's something that I'm often told by friends and family, "Fran, you're too nice". That's why I have been hurt so many times because people take advantage of my love and my generosity.

For me, love is a feeling that just bubbles up and needs to be shared, as if my heart is overflowing with warmth and compassion. And when I'm lucky enough to see a smile in return, it brings me so much joy and satisfaction. All I ever want is to see people happy and if I can contribute to that, then I'll do whatever I can to succeed in the happiness of others.

Whenever I'm presented with an opportunity to show someone kindness, no matter how small or insignificant it may seem at the time, I take it without hesitation. It's what I do naturally. This is like my default setting. From simply holding the door for somebody entering a building, or saying hi to strangers on a motorbike night, these tiny moments make all the difference in my life. Not only do they force me to take notice of people from different backgrounds and perspectives, but they also give me the opportunity to express appreciation for their presence in my life; ultimately allowing me to feel connected.

I have learned to express more love, affection, compassion, and empathy to others. If we can share our love with others, then surely the world will be a much nicer place. Remember in Chapter five, where I told you how Faye wished I was dead? Well, I have been doing everything I can to never hear those words ever again. Things are so much better now. I have such a strong relationship with Faye. Not, just Faye, I also have a strong relationship with Sara and in fact, their mother as well. I have put measures in place to mitigate the risk of comments like that ever happening. I love and respect those amazing girls too much to jeopardise the powerful relationship we now have.

The power of love is something that cannot be understated; both giving and receiving it have profound effects on our lives and those around us. As Mahatma Gandhi once said, *"Where there is love there is life"*. These words will continue to guide me through life, as long as there are people to share my love with.

Growth

Growth is massive in my life. It's what I truly stand for. If you're not growing, you're dying, and I'm certainly not in the mindset of the latter. For me, growth is about looking within and finding areas of your life and doing whatever it takes to be the best in all of these areas. By putting in the work and investing in yourself, this means you will have a 10 out of 10 in every area of your life. Hence living your best life…being the best version of you. As you may have noticed throughout this book, I am very passionate about personal growth.

Freedom

For me, personal freedom is one of my top core values following authenticity and I believe it is how we all should live our lives. Freedom means something different for everyone but for me, it's all about living my life on my terms. It includes a range of aspects of my life such as being in complete control of my own destiny, financial freedom, time freedom, geographical freedom and more.

Financial freedom is one of the most important components of personal freedom, as it allows us to choose how we want to earn and spend our money, without feeling restricted by financial obligations. For example, having financial independence can open up new career opportunities or allow people to pursue goals that may have been previously out of reach, due to a lack of resources. It means making money work for you, instead of you working for money all the time in a 9-to-5 corporate job. It also means being able to provide for yourself and your family without worrying about scarcity of money or not being able to pay bills. In other words, being self-reliant and self-sufficient. I have learned to focus on diversification, and not putting all of my eggs into one basket. I invested in teaching myself how to create multiple streams of income so that I could protect myself and my family by being recession-proof. I never ever want to rely on one source of income anymore, as I believe it's simply too risky. Experiencing multiple job losses has taught me that valuable lesson in life, which is now a big part of my vision…financial freedom.

Time freedom is the most important element of personal freedom, because it allows us more control over how we use our time. Time is the most precious asset that we all have, and it can never be replaced. As an example, someone who has time freedom may be able to take an extended holiday or pursue a side project without worrying about taking time away from work commitments or responsibilities. Time independence also gives us the opportunity for more quality moments with our loved ones, or to take up a passion project. I have many passion projects as part of the vision, which is why managing my time is essential.

Achieving time and financial freedom automatically qualifies us to live a life with geographical freedom. Money and time in abundance give us the power to choose where we want to live and work, how many holidays we go on, and so on. Having all three of these elements to me is living the ultimate lifestyle. And this is what I strive for in life…personal freedom.

Transformation

Standing for life transformation involves going from one state (normally negative) to another (positive) and that is something I truly believe in. This can be in the form of many things, such as a mindset shift, a career change, a complete lifestyle change, how you are in relationships and around family and friends. The most important thing is wanting and committing to the transformation. Like I said before, if we're static and not growing, then there is no chance of gaining the transformation we dream of. So for me, transformation means everything if we want to strive to be the highest and best version of ourselves.

CHAPTER NINE

BREAKTHROUGH

Now that you have read all of my rejection and abandonment experiences, and what I believe in, I thought it was time to now look at some of the solutions to this. What I mean by this, is how do we actually overcome rejection and the fear that is associated with rejection and abandonment?

There are several strategies that can be used to help us move past this. Personally, I did not want to be carrying this weight on my shoulders for the rest of my life, wondering and guessing when and where the next traumatic rejection moment was coming. I had to fight this fear of rejection head-on, get the breakthrough that I wanted, and live the happy, joyful life that I deserve.

Instead of being defined by tragedy, and traumatic experiences, I decided to define myself through my reaction. In a way, rejection has given me a new lease on life and turned a story of tragedy into one filled with joy and meaning. My mission is now to inspire millions of people to shift their perspective on what 'rejection' means and to turn adverse circumstances into strength and motivation. In other words, choosing happiness, instead of choosing to be the victim of our own story.

So, the most important thing to remember is that although the feelings associated with rejection and abandonment are real, they will eventually pass if you apply these strategies and tactics that I'm about to share with you. It is integral for individuals to practice self-care during this time and trust the process.

Strategy #1 – Connection

Surround yourself with people you want to become, the people who build you up. People who inspire you, encourage and love you no matter what you do. Seeking support from family or friends is a must do. There is no negotiation with this one. Family and close friends will always be there for you.

When I was in a dark place, which happened many times, the first thing I would do is reach out for support. Living on the ninth-floor apartment, above a hotel in the centre of a city and jumping out of my window felt like an easy way out. Fortunately, due to the safety window, this was not possible and is actually the thing that saved me that day. Putting that post on Facebook was another life-saver. This was a cry for help as I didn't know what else to do. I had to share my feelings with my loved ones, as I didn't want to face this alone. The reaction I got was incredible…People who went to primary school with me, nearly thirty years earlier, were reaching out to me asking me if I was okay. The level of support was amazing. I was literally blown away by the number of people who took the time out of their day to read my post, and reached out to me, to offer their love and support. I felt so blessed, knowing that I was not on my own. I have so many great friends and the best family, who have always been there for me.

I just didn't know it or appreciate the love and support that was already there in front of my eyes. I experienced a lot of gratitude from that day. I'm not saying you have to put a post on Facebook to find the answer, but it's more about leaning on your family and friends for support and talking to them for guidance and comfort. I simply could not have done this on my own. Your family is always there for you, even if you think they're not.

Another method I discovered for a true connection is to host a virtual summit. A virtual summit is simply an interview series. This is where you become the host of your own show and interview like-minded people, or expert speakers from all over the world. You choose the topic and you choose the format. The topic can be anything from personal development, mindset, to business development and entrepreneurial strategies. The format can be either a live event or pre-recorded. A live event is where you interview everyone on your panel in one session in a zoom meeting. Pre-recorded is when you interview everyone individually. This is a one-on-one call between you and your expert speakers.

I discovered this method of connecting with successful people when I invested in a community of entrepreneurs. I am now running many virtual summits around the topic of rejection and abandonment, learning so many new insights and other strategies that I can implement into my own life and share with others. The best thing about virtual summits is that you don't need any qualifications, any previous experience, or even a credible website. All you need is the passion, commitment and determination to just get started.

It was on my first pre-recorded virtual summit, where I connected with Annie Gibbins, the founder and CEO of my book publishing company, Women's Biz Global. I interviewed the incredible Annie in October 2022 around the topic of having a growth mindset, and what strategies she uses in her businesses and personal life. It was a fascinating and lovely conversation and one I will never forget. I am now blessed to be working with her and her extraordinary publishing company. This connection has been life-changing.

Strategy #2 – Acceptance

Rejection and abandonment are two of the most painful emotional experiences a person can endure. Yet, it's an experience that many face and try to navigate. Understanding and acknowledging the emotions associated with rejection and abandonment is essential for coping with these difficult situations and it can provide some relief, as well a sense of control over our circumstances.

Rejection can occur in many forms, from romantic relationships to losing a job, or even something as simple as being excluded from a social group, as I know too well. It's normal to feel devastated after a rejection, especially if it has been ongoing for some time. You might feel worthless, hurt and lonely after experiencing rejection, as you may come to believe that you were only rejected because you weren't good enough, or weren't liked by others. This was how I felt.

Some common emotions experienced during and after rejections include fear of further rejections, sadness, anger, shame, anxiety, depression and trauma. People also often have difficulty understanding why they were rejected, which can further add to their pain. It is important that if you are struggling with feelings of rejection to be mindful that how you feel is valid - it doesn't make you weak - but instead, it provides you with strength to heal from these hard moments in life. I didn't realise how strong I was until I started understanding and acknowledging these emotions. It may not feel like it, but you have so much strength and power inside of you.

Abandonment has similar effects on people's emotional wellbeing, yet can be far more intense due to its extreme nature. Abandonment usually occurs when someone leaves us suddenly or unexpectedly without any explanation or sense of closure, which makes it incredibly difficult to process what happened and why we were left behind. The person or family who was abandoned might feel like they don't matter. When a relationship unfortunately comes to an end, the person who was abandoned might feel like they won't ever find love again because of their previous experience, which can lead to intense emotional distress including feelings of despair, loneliness, confusion, and betrayal. Having experienced different forms of abandonment, I know exactly what emotions come with abandonment. But just remember this, you are worthy.

If you're struggling with feelings of rejection or abandonment and want to move forward in life, it is important to understand that these emotions are natural responses when faced with traumatic situations. Learning how to accept our own emotions and cope with them in healthy ways will help you better understand what happened, while also learning how best to process the experience moving forward. Self-care, such as talking through the emotions with a professional therapist, or leaning on trusted friends and family members, will provide invaluable support during this time period and aid in healing eventually leading to positive personal growth over time.

It's important to remember that there are other people who have gone through similar experiences. So, developing connections will allow you to know that there is hope on the other side of this difficult situation.

That's why I thought it was fitting to name this book, 'Abandonment to Acceptance,' as this is the transformation. We go from a state of loneliness and pain, not having all the answers, to a state of acceptance, recognising it for what it is and moving forward in life with no more pain and suffering. Instead, you feel at peace with yourself and develop self-love in abundance.

Strategy #3 - Strive for success

Success is something that we all strive for. But what does it really mean to be successful? Is it simply achieving our goals, or is there more to it than that?

How do you define success? The definition below is my version of personal success. Yours may be very different. Success means something very different for us all.

"Success is having the courage, commitment, and growth mindset to invest in myself, facing my fears, working smarter, building a temple of wealth, where I live a fulfilled life of self-reliance, personal freedom, and flexibility in abundance, doing the things that really matter to me...standing for growth, freedom, and transformation, having a positive impact on the world, transforming millions of people's lives with authenticity, love, peace and connection with a lasting generational legacy." - Fran Wilson

I believe that we all have the power and potential within us to create our own variation of success. There is no one definition. Your version of success might look completely different from mine. See it as the DNA of your story, your journey.

Just remember this...if you quit, you fail. So, keep on striving to create the successful life that you want.

"Success depends upon previous preparation, and without such preparation there is sure to be failure." – Confucius

Strategy #4 - Persistent action

Persistence is one of the most important keys to success, both in business and in life. Anyone who has ever achieved anything noteworthy has done so because they were willing to keep going, even when the going got tough. Just think about any goal you've ever set for yourself - whether it was losing weight, quitting smoking, or starting your own business. It's highly unlikely that you achieved that goal after the first attempt. More likely, it took multiple efforts and a lot of persistence to finally reach your goal.

I know that's what I experienced with my weight loss program during the lockdown in 2020. Of course, I didn't see the results after one day…It took weeks, actually months, of persistent and consistent action and effort to start seeing the results I wanted. I reached my goal after six months and I never felt better. I must admit, that was the best I've ever felt in my life. All that effort had paid off. But more importantly, it was because of my mindset shift to make it happen. That really is the secret to success.

With persistence, it is possible to overcome any obstacle and achieve any goal. This is especially true in business, where growth can be slow and difficult. But those who persevere always find a way to succeed in the end. Businesses that are able to maintain a growth mindset and continue pushing forward, even in the face of adversity, are more likely to achieve long-term success, as they are able to build a loyal customer-base and establish a strong reputation.

The same is true for personal growth. It is only through persistent action and effort that we are able to make lasting changes in our lives. With a persistent mindset, anything is possible. So if you want to create long-term sustainable success, never give up and always keep moving forward.

"It does not matter how slowly you go as long as you do not stop." – Confucius

Strategy #5 - Consistent hard work

Consistent hard work is another key to sustainable success. It's easy to get caught up in the day-to-day grind and lose sight of the long-term goal, but consistent effort will always pay off in the end. The most successful people in any field are usually the ones who have put in the most consistent effort over time. They never quit, even when things were tough. They stayed focused and kept growing, learning new things, and pushing themselves to be better.

This consistent hard work ethic is what separates them from the rest. It's not always easy, but it's always worth it. With a consistent work ethic and a growth mindset, anything is possible. Like I said in regards to my weight loss program, that would never have happened if I wasn't consistent with the program steps every single day (doing body weight workouts, calorie counting and walking ten thousand steps a day).

If you want to be successful and overcome adversity, never give up and never quit working hard. Stay focused, consistent, and always strive to improve. You'll get there in the end if you never give up on yourself.

"A dream doesn't become reality through magic; it takes sweat, determination and hard work." - Colin Powell

Strategy #6 - Create daily habits

Another method to overcome the fear of rejection is to create new daily habits. Creating new habits can be difficult, but it's worth it in the long run. In the end, creating new habits is all about setting yourself up for success in the long term. By taking the time to develop new habits, you are investing in your future and ensuring that you will be able to achieve your goals.

According to a 2009 study published in the European Journal of Social Psychology, it can take anywhere from 18 to 254 days for a person to form a new habit and **an average of 76 days for a new behaviour to become automatic**.

There's no one-size-fits-all figure, which is why this time frame is so broad; some habits are easier to form than others, and some people may find it easier to develop new behaviours. There is no right or wrong timeline. The only timeline that matters is the one that works best for you.

If you think about it, one habit we all have is brushing our teeth when we wake up in the morning and just before we go to bed at night. This habit was formed from a very young age and enforced by our parents. Now we do it without even thinking about it. This is just one of many examples we're all generally aware of.

One of the most important aspects of creating new daily habits is what I have just mentioned…consistency. This also means that we need to be disciplined in carrying out our new routines each day, especially in the morning. It's often said that the early bird catches the worm, and this is very true. Many successful people have a morning ritual that they follow religiously, which sets them up for a productive day. They might meditate, exercise, review their goals, or read inspiring material. Whatever it is, their morning routine gives them a mental and physical boost that helps them tackle the challenges of the day ahead.

Of course, not every new habit needs to be related to successful and wealthy people. Creating healthy habits such as eating breakfast, getting enough sleep, and spending time with loved ones, are all important for sustaining a healthy mind, body and lifestyle in the long term.

One of the best resources I found for creating a new morning routine and a daily habit is, 'The Miracle Morning - The Six Habits That Will Transform Your Life Before 8am,' by Hal Elrod [4]. What if you could wake up tomorrow and EVERY area of your life was beginning to transform, what would you change? 'The Miracle Morning' is already transforming the lives of tens of thousands of people around the world by showing them how to wake up each day with more ENERGY, MOTIVATION and FOCUS, to take your life to the next level. Hal's book has helped me to create structure to my morning and really set myself up for the day, and it did this by giving me a proven strategy where I focus on six different productive activities, known as S.A.V.E.R.S.

Silence / Meditation
Affirmation
Visualisation
Exercise
Reading
Scribing

Here is my S.A.V.E.R.S routine:

04:55am - I wake up feeling positive
05:00am - I meditate for 10 minutes **(S)**
05:10am - I say my positive affirmations to myself in the mirror **(A)**
05:20am - I visualise my ideal life and vision for my future **(V)**
05:30am - I do a bodyweight workout for a toned upper body **(E)**
05:40am - I listen to motivational and personal development audio books **(R)**
05:50am - I journal in my diary with things I'm grateful for **(S)**
06:00am - I'm feeling energised and ready for the day!

This has really helped me take my mind off rejection and focus on my own happiness and productivity instead, even before my day begins. Sometimes the fear of rejection suppresses everything else in our lives. For me, I got to a point where I had lost my identity, and creating these new habits was critical for me to re-discover who I truly was. No matter what new habit you're trying to create, remember to be patient and consistent, and you'll eventually achieve your goal.

"Your net worth to the world is usually determined by what remains after your bad habits are subtracted from your good ones." - Benjamin Franklin

Strategy #7 - Overcoming failures

For anyone striving for success, I believe failure is not an option. I really do believe this. However, failures in life are inevitable and it's important to accept this fact. Therefore, a growth mindset is essential for long-term sustainable success. This means that you must be willing to try again after a failure occurs and believe that you can improve with each attempt. It's also important to acknowledge your failures. Accepting failures and acknowledging them are essential for learning from mistakes and growing as an individual. By doing so, you create a strong foundation for sustainable success.

Despite what some people may think, failure is not the opposite of success...it is a part of it. Failure breeds resilience and a growth mindset. Resilience is the ability to recover from, or adjust easily to, misfortune or change. It's what allows us to pick ourselves up after we've been knocked down and try again. I know this too well. I never knew how resilient I was until I went through all of the rejections in my life. I felt I had no choice but to pick myself up from all of those job losses and to go again. Quitting simply wasn't an option for me...Yes it was stressful, but I had to keep moving forward.

A growth mindset, on the other hand, is the belief that failure is not final, that it's possible to grow and learn from our mistakes. This mindset is what allows us to see failure or even a crisis as an opportunity to learn and improve, rather than as an insurmountable obstacle. A great example of this was the devastating COVID pandemic we all endured. Obviously, this was a global crisis, but it created so many opportunities, such as businesses pivoting and adapting to more online events and people given the opportunity to work from home, which meant spending more time with their families. Schools adapted and converted their educational material to a digital format. This was particularly a whole new experience for my two daughters, Faye and Sara.

It's moments like these that we need to remember that just because the rug has been pulled from under us, it does not mean we have to give up and quit. Instead, we can adapt, pivot, be creative, and innovative.

So, next time something doesn't work out the way you want it, or you're faced with an obstacle or traumatic experience, please whatever you do, don't quit – try again, keep going, but do things differently. I have learned so many lessons from my failed relationships and multiple job losses. It has made me develop new boundaries in life and to set significantly higher standards in my life. I now have a zero-tolerance to being disrespected.
If you quit, you fail.

"Many of life's failures are people who did not realise how close they were to success when they gave up." Thomas A. Edison

Strategy #8 – Discipline

Discipline is another essential tool for achieving long-term success. It enables you to manage your mind, develop a code of behaviour and follow best practices. It also helps you to adhere to standards and policies.

The benefits of discipline include improved performance, increased productivity and reduced stress. Furthermore, it can help you to achieve your goals and reach your full potential. A lack of discipline can lead to procrastination, frustration and disappointment.

When you're disciplined, you're less likely to be swayed by short-term temptation or peer pressure. You're more likely to stick to your guns, even when things get tough. And it's this quality that separates successful people, from those who never quite manage to realise their potential.

Also, when you're disciplined, you don't allow your emotions to control your actions. You think before you act, and you stick to your code of behaviour, no matter what. This allows you to stay focused on your goals and follow through with your plans.

I'm sure you can think of many times when you were so disciplined in order to complete a task in your life. For me, one that sticks out the most is the weight loss program that I previously mentioned. Without this discipline, I would never have lost so much weight. And this is what it comes down to…how much do you want to achieve your goal? For me, losing weight was non-negotiable. It was my mission to look and feel good. If you want to achieve long-term success, you need to develop and maintain a high level of discipline.

"To enjoy good health, to bring true happiness to one's family, to bring peace to all, one must first discipline and control one's own mind. If a man can control his mind he can find the way to Enlightenment, and all wisdom and virtue will naturally come to him." — Buddha

Strategy #9 – Sacrifice

To achieve long-term sustainable success, it's often necessary to make sacrifices. This may involve giving up some of your free time, or sacrificing your social life to focus on your goals. While it can be difficult to make these changes, they're often exactly what's needed to achieve your objectives. One of the most important things to remember when making sacrifices is that they should be based on your values and priorities. If you value your family and friends above all else, which I'm sure you do, then sacrificing time with them, in order to work on your career may not be the best decision. However, if you have a clear understanding of what you want to achieve, then making sacrifices in other areas of your life can help you to focus on your goals and achieve them.

It's also important to keep in mind that not all sacrifices have to be permanent. If you find that you are struggling to balance work and your personal life, then it may be necessary to make some adjustments in the short-term. The key is to make sure that your sacrifices are based on your overall goals and objectives, and not simply on what is convenient in the moment. By making sacrifices now, we can lay the foundation for a bright future.

"The only question to ask yourself is, how much are you willing to sacrifice to achieve this success?" - Larry Flynt

Strategy #10 - Managing criticism

Criticism is a part of life, especially when you're striving to improve yourself. Whether it's criticism from family, friends, or strangers, negative comments can be hard to take. It's important to remember that not everyone will agree with your choices or understand your motives. When you're criticised, try to see it as an opportunity to learn and grow.

Take the time to listen to what the other person has to say. They may have valid points that can help you improve. If you feel like the criticism is unwarranted or unfair, don't be afraid to stand up for yourself. Remember, you're the only one who knows what is best for you. Don't let other people's judgement cloud your own perspective. At the end of the day, you're the one who has to live with your choices.

I have been criticised many times in my life, around my choices, and my decisions to reskill and learn how to adapt and pivot with the rapidly changing world we live in. Yes, the criticism does hurt. It's hard enough to make a change in your life, but when people you love and trust criticise you, it feels impossible. But I'm actually grateful for the criticism, because it's made me who I am today. I'm stronger and more determined than ever to succeed. And I will never give up on my dreams and neither should you.

The key is how you handle criticism. If you let it get to you, then it can damage your self-esteem and make you feel bad about yourself. However, if you take criticism in your stride and use it as an opportunity to learn and improve, then it can be a positive experience. The next time you receive criticism, take a deep breath and remind yourself that not everyone is going to agree with you all the time. Then, use the criticism to your advantage by learning from it and making the necessary changes.

"The final proof of greatness lies in being able to endure criticism without resentment." - Elbert Hubbard

Strategy #11 - Overcoming self-doubt

Doubts can have a major impact on the decisions we make in life. When we are self-doubtful, we tend to second-guess ourselves and our abilities. This can lead us to make decisions that are based more on fear than on logic. Similarly, when we are uncertain about something, we may be reluctant to act. We may also worry that we'll make the wrong decision and end up regretting it. Doubts can cause us to hesitate and delay making decisions, even when doing so would be in our best interest. In other words, procrastination kicks in. In many cases, the best way to overcome doubts is to simply take a leap of faith and trust our instincts. By doing so, we can learn to listen to our inner voice and make decisions that are true to ourselves.

We all face self-doubt at some point in our lives. Whether we're making a decision about our career, our relationships, or our future, self-doubt can creep in and make us second-guess ourselves. This can leave us feeling uncertain and worried that we're making the wrong choice. Self-doubt can be paralysing, preventing us from taking any action at all. We may become reluctant to take risks, for fear of failure or disappointment. However, self-doubt can also be a motivating force, pushing us to work harder and strive for excellence.

Ultimately, self-doubt is part of the human experience. It's normal to feel unsure or apprehensive about life choices. What's important is how we deal with self-doubt. Do we let it control us, like those voices in our head that I mentioned earlier, or do we use it as a tool to help us make better decisions? When we learn to embrace self-doubt, it can become so powerful on the journey of life. Remember, you're the only one who can decide what is best for your life. Trust yourself and don't let self-doubt keep you from living the life you want to live, or it will sabotage your momentum towards success.

"Some of our important choices have a timeline.
If we delay a decision, the opportunity is gone forever. Sometimes our doubts
keep us from making a choice that involves change. Thus an opportunity may
be missed." - James E. Faust

Strategy #12 – Courage

Courage is another essential quality that can have a profound impact on our lives. It takes courage to stand up for what we believe in, even when we're faced with opposition. It takes courage to pursue our dreams, even when the path ahead is uncertain. And it takes courage to face our fears, even when they seem insurmountable.

I must admit, I didn't realise how courageous I actually am. Over the years, I discovered through my journey in life, I have many experiences that scared me to death, and pushed me way out of my comfort zone. It's amazing what you learn about yourself when you commit to something. I have proven to myself and my loved ones how much courage I have within me. The first experience was when I moved from Dublin to the UK on my own in 2003, when I was only 20 years old. I'm not going to lie, I didn't think I would last. However, over 20 years later, I now know I can go and do anything I put my mind to.

The other biggest experience I would consider showing my high level of courage, was when I invested in myself. Not many people know this, but I took out a secured loan on my house, which I used to invest in personal development and business development programs. This included travelling to the Gold Coast, in Australia for ten days, where I connected with like-minded entrepreneurs.

When we summon the courage to do these things, we open ourselves up to new possibilities and new experiences. We also send a message to the world that we are not afraid to take risks and that we're willing to stand up for what we believe in. Courage is a powerful quality that can change our lives for the better.

Courage is not a trait that we are born with. It is something that we develop over time through our experiences. And the more courageous we are, the more capable we are of handling whatever life throws our way, such as multiple job losses or toxic relationships. So, if you ever find yourself in need of some courage, remember that it is always within you, you already have it, it's just waiting to be unleashed.

"I learned that courage was not the absence of fear, but the triumph over it. The brave man is not he who does not feel afraid, but he who conquers that fear." - Nelson Mandela

Strategy #13 - Master your mindset

Creating change and shifting your mindset is also a necessary part of life if you want to create success and design the life you want. We create change through the allowance of our painful emotions, such as boredom, irritation, frustration, anxiety, anger, jealousy, sadness, guilt and depression. We also create change through a mindset shift. There are two approaches to this. The first is when you have a mindset of judgement. Your critical thoughts towards yourself, others and external conditions, which ensures that you are in emotional pain, meaning you're either living in the past or fretting about the future in a negative way.

The other approach is when you allow your emotional pain, accept your emotional pain and create opposite thoughts towards yourself, others and external conditions, ensuring that you're in these emotions, which include happiness, confidence, motivation, forgiveness, compassion, acceptance and calmness. You can take the relevant actions to create change. This ensures you're living in the now. If you want to create change, allow, accept and align with the aforementioned pains. This in turn creates a shift of frequency and then shifts the thought you're having towards yourself, others and external conditions. You will feel better and know that change comes from this place. However, if you cannot create change of external conditions, at least you'll feel better about it and feel a sense of happiness, confidence, motivation, forgiveness, compassion, acceptance and calmness.

Obviously, it can be very difficult to change your mindset. It doesn't happen overnight, but it's worth it in the end. The reason for writing this book was to prove to myself and the world that I no longer accept being bullied, controlled, and manipulated by others. Change had to happen for me…it was non-negotiable. It was time to take full control of my emotions.

And you have the power to do the very same. A small change can make a big difference. It takes time and effort, but if you're willing to put in the work, you can achieve transformation, and a truly joyful and happy life by your own design. Every marathon starts with the first step, and the first step is always the hardest. A positive mindset is an important part of life. It's what can take us away from living a mediocre life, to living an extraordinary life.

Do you want to just settle and live a mediocre life? I doubt it.

Without change, we would be stuck in the same place, never moving forward, living a boring mediocre life. Do you want to just survive or powerfully thrive? Transformation is what happens when we make changes in our lives. It is a process that can be gradual or sudden, but it always results in some type of personal growth. This is something I'm hugely passionate about. I stand for growth, freedom and transformation.

"If we're not growing and blossoming, we're dying" -
Fran Wilson

When we commit to transformation, we often find that our lives become more fulfilling and meaningful. We may also discover new talents and abilities that we never knew we had. It's amazing what you can learn about yourself in such a short time. While going through that emotional bullying from Lauren, I somehow found the strength, and of course, courage to invest in a transformation and leadership community that taught me about mindset.

I learned how to build my own interview series and I worked nonstop to interview twenty-eight people, including millionaires, around the world on the topic of having a growth mindset. I was relentless and kept going, as life transformation meant so much to me. It still does and always will do. We should never stop learning about ourselves and what we're capable of.

Happiness comes from within…it's a choice, and it's often the result of making positive changes in our lives. If we focus on our goals and priorities, we are more likely to achieve them. My problem in life was that I had always been driven by the negative results, which defined my lack of happiness. I never focused on the good things that were right in front of me.

Success leaves clues, and it comes from having a balance in all areas of your life: health, wealth, self and social. When one area is out of balance, it can have a negative impact on the others. To create a life of joy and happiness, you must focus on all four areas and make sure that they are all in equilibrium. This may take time, but it is worth the effort. Creating success in your life requires making changes, sometimes big and sometimes small. But always remember that even a small change can make a big difference.

"One reason people resist change is because they focus on what they have to give up, instead of what they have to gain." - Rick Godwin

Strategy #14 - Take risks

In order to be successful, you have to be willing to take risks. This means that you need to have a brave mindset and be willing to step out of your comfort zone. It can be terrifying to do things that make you feel uncomfortable, but it is essential for growth. By taking risks, you're showing strength and proving to yourself that you can do whatever it takes to achieve your goals.

It is also important to have a no-fear attitude when it comes to taking risks. This means that you should not let your fears hold you back from doing what you want or from achieving success. Instead, you should face your fears head-on and use them as motivation to keep moving forward. If you want to be successful, you must take risks and have a 'Do Whatever It Takes' mindset.

Risk-takers are often rewarded for their bravery with opportunities for growth and new experiences. If you're stuck in a rut, it may be time to take some risks and push yourself out of your comfort zone. Remember, no one ever achieved greatness by playing it safe. Be brave, be strong, and most importantly, don't be afraid to fail. Failures are simply steps on the road to success.

Personally, I have taken many risks on my journey to success. I wouldn't be where I am today if I didn't commit to big risks. As I have just said, the biggest risk I've taken was to take out a secured loan against my house. My "Why" was simply too big not to do this. I sold that house so I could invest even more equity into my future…personal development and growth.

I am certainly a risk-taker. Nothing can stop me from creating the life I want, even toxic and controlling people as I have now learned how to handle this abuse and rejection.

"The only way to discover the limits of the possible is to go beyond them into the impossible." - Arthur C. Clarke

Strategy #15 - Remove negativity

Remove it...Remove it...Remove it...

One of the best things you can do for yourself is to remove negative people and influences from your life. These negative forces can come in the form of toxic friends, partners, destructive family members, or even strangers who make negative comments. This negativity can be very hurtful and distracting, and it can negatively impact your self-confidence, as I'm sure you know.

However, by removing these negative influences from your life, you can refocus your energy on achieving your goals. Additionally, you may find that you're better able to handle criticism when it comes from a positive place. So don't be afraid to cut out the negative people and influences in your life - it's one of the best decisions you can make for yourself. For me, I got to choose to no longer have controlling and manipulating people in my life. For example, my ex-partner of over five years. As I have mentioned before, I only surround myself with the people I want to become, and she is not one of them. It may sound harsh but I must protect myself and remain within integrity.

"Success is falling nine times and getting up ten." – Jon Bon Jovi

Strategy #16 - Discover your purpose

So, what is a purpose? Every human being has a unique skill and gift. Your purpose is your God-given talent and go serve it to the world. This should be something that you would absolutely love to do, such as your career dream, and what you've got to do is recognise what your strengths and talents are and find a way to unleash it to the world.

So, for me, my purpose in life is to openly and honestly give others the support to recognise and appreciate their value so that they are inspired to adapt and passionately build a proud legacy.

Everybody has their unique gift and I want you to have patience when searching for it. Sometimes your purpose isn't revealed for a while. Once you find your purpose, give your whole heart and soul to it, and enjoy the journey, enjoy the fulfilment, as well as the absolute joy that you have from within, as you serve your gift outwards. Trust me, your unique gift will come. Unleash that power within.

"Our prime purpose in this life is to help others. And if you can't help them, at least don't hurt them." – Dalai Lama

Strategy #17 - Choose love

Choose love…choose self-love…

The path to true inner peace and happiness starts within. That's why it's so important to choose love for ourselves, even when life throws us into situations where we may feel overwhelmed or uncertain. Choosing self-love in these times can be incredibly difficult, but it's essential if we want to live a fulfilled and meaningful life.

Self-love is an act of compassion towards ourselves and our own well-being. It isn't about narcissism or conceit, it's about acknowledging our own worth and believing that we deserve happiness and success. Self-love can take many forms, from taking time for yourself in between work commitments, to indulging in a hobby you enjoy, or spending quality time with family and friends.

One of the most powerful ways to practice self-love is through positive affirmations. Positive affirmations are uplifting statements that help us focus on the good things about ourselves and give us strength when facing adversity. These affirmations can be repeated throughout the day or whenever needed, as a reminder of our strength and potential. Examples include, "I am capable of achieving my goals," or "I have everything I need for success," or "I am worthy." Remember the S.A.V.E.R.S routine that I mentioned in strategy #6? Well the "A" is the affirmation, and this is a great opportunity in your morning routine to express these positive statements about yourself. This is powerful.

It's also important to remember that self-love isn't something that will happen overnight; rather it is a process that takes time, effort, and dedication to cultivate real changes in our lives. Start building your self-love practice today. Get into a new habit and set aside some time each day for yourself...even if it's just five minutes. Close your eyes, go within, and listen to what your body needs at this moment in time, without judgement or expectation.

Finally, remember that no one else can determine our worth; only we have the power to choose love for ourselves every day. With conscious effort and care, you too can unlock the full power of choosing love in all aspects of your life. I felt it was fitting that I use the "A Hero's Journey To Self-Love" subtitle for this book. We are all on our unique journey, and we are all heroes. You are a powerful hero and I want you to reach that destination of self-love that you deserve.

"I believe that every single event in life happens in an opportunity to choose love over fear." – Oprah Winfrey

Strategy #18 - Choose happiness

Happiness is a choice. It is an attitude and a way of life, not something that is determined by our circumstances. Many of us may believe that money, relationships and success are the key to happiness, but the truth is that these things can only bring temporary joy. This was certainly how I felt for most of my life. I was codependent and believed that I would be happy in the perfect loving relationship, with the perfect job. However, happiness is always there within us and to find true lasting happiness, we must look within ourselves and make conscious choices to live a life full of positive thoughts, meaningful relationships, and a sense of purpose. It truly is about having a positive attitude.

On the surface, reaching for moments of pleasure may appear to be a path towards happiness. However, this type of short-term gratification will quickly fade and leave us feeling even more empty than before. Instead of seeking out external sources for validation or satisfaction, it is important to turn inward for contentment. In other words, work on yourself and work on self-love. When we take time to nurture our inner being, with activities such as meditation or mindfulness exercises, we can create a steady foundation for long-term happiness.

Our attitude plays an essential role in fostering positivity in our lives as well. We have the power to choose how we react to any situation, whether it's positive or negative, depending on your individual mindset. This has been the biggest challenge for me personally, but I have learned to operate with a mindset shift and create a positive attitude with gratitude in abundance. If we focus on developing an optimistic outlook on life, rather than wallowing in self-pity or despair, it can have a tremendous impact on our overall state of well-being, because we can then be the person we were born to be and truly live a joyful and happy life with no barriers or limitations In other words, we get out of our head and get out of our own way.

To achieve genuine joy in life, it is also essential that we invest in meaningful relationships with those around us. Building trust and forming connections with those who share similar values can provide immense support during difficult times and increase our sense of belonging. Keep your circle of friends small, but very strong. Furthermore, surrounding yourself with encouraging people will help foster healthy habits that contribute to your overall mental health and wellbeing. As I have stated before, connect with the people who inspire you, raise your frequency, and who you want to become. When you surround yourself with your tribe, the energy is electric and positive energy flows in abundance. This connection makes you feel a real sense of happiness.

Lastly, having a sense of purpose or direction gives us something bigger than ourselves to strive towards, and helps cultivate motivation throughout every aspect of life. Whether it's teaching others about the importance of diversification or dedicating time towards volunteer work in a charity organisation, knowing why you're doing something makes all the difference when it comes to staying happy and fulfilled, instead of relying solely on material gain for satisfaction.

Ultimately, determining what brings you true contentment is a process that will evolve as your interests change and grow...but one thing should always remain constant...your commitment towards living an authentic life based on what truly matters most to you, rather than externally sourced gratification from those around you. You do not need to look for validation from others to live your life. Taking control over your own destiny through mindful decision-making ultimately leads down the road towards genuine lifelong happiness. I know that following this path requires dedication and self-belief, but trust me, it yields amazing rewards!

Let me explain the unhappy mindset behaviours versus happy mindset and behaviours. Let's look at a scenario of two different people. Person number one is someone who is chasing happiness. They're always focused on external conditions changing and because of this, they're stressed or in a control mode via attachment and non-accepting thoughts. They believe they will be happy when something changes in their external world. Yes, they might feel happy if they get their PhD, sports car, or earn their first million. They'll be happy for a few days, or weeks, but then they're going to go back to chasing happiness, and let me tell you, it's a controlling place. They remain attached to external validation via relationship, sources, and substances and they might have judgmental critical or blaming thoughts, which create frustration and anger. There's a huge lack of accountability for their thoughts, emotions, and behaviours, creating a victim mindset, and they might become focused on the past in a depressed and regretful way, or view the future in an anxious way, which in turn creates unhappiness.

Whereas person number two has done some self-development work, and they know that happiness is here right now. It is in alignment with the now and so they accept external conditions with gratitude. Some external conditions we cannot change, so they choose to not let it worry them. They choose to feel peaceful, calm, motivated and centred. They pursue their goals, but from a happy and grateful place. The achievement of their goals doesn't define their self-esteem. This person is focused on internal validation, which ensures they have high self-respect, high self-esteem, high self-confidence, and are focused on joyful, compassionate, loving, blissful thoughts. They take accountability for their thoughts, emotions, and behaviours and they're focused on the now…happiness is here in the now.

"Happiness can exist only in acceptance." – *George Orwell*

Strategy #19 - Be grateful

Following on from what I was just talking about, let's look at gratitude. Probably the most important ways of being. Being grateful for the things we have in life gets taken for granted every single day. We must remember and appreciate all of the things we have in life, no matter how small or insignificant we think they might be.

The power of gratitude lies in its ability to bring us back into the present moment, which in my opinion, is the only place where we can truly experience joy. We do this by recalling our blessings, instead of worrying about what happened, what might have been, or what might lie ahead. By recognising even the smallest successes or kindnesses experienced during our day-to-day lives, from finding a free parking space near the beach, like I do all the time, to receiving a small gift outside my door from a neighbour unexpectedly. We can find moments of joy throughout our days that remind us how much there is still left for us to be grateful for, no matter how challenging things may seem at times. Gratitude does not get rid of the challenges we face or bring back what we may have lost, instead it is a tool that enables us to appreciate what we do have. Even receiving a hug from a loved one can make all the difference and triggers so much gratitude in someone. I must say, I do appreciate a hug, and of course, I offer great hugs myself!

If you wake up and you start having negative thoughts such as, "Man, this ain't my day", "Do I have to work?", "I don't feel like doing anything," every time you feel yourself doing that…stop, just stop for a second, and start going over in your mind everything you have to be grateful for. Not everything you want, but everything you already have. Because what you have is substantial. You just haven't gone over the list and taken inventory in a long time. But the fact that you can walk, that's a blessing. The fact that you woke up this morning, that's another blessing. The fact that you can see, think, and reason, that's another blessing. The fact that you have access to food is again another substantial blessing. I could give you fifty things you should be grateful for right now without even knowing you. Start thinking this way, and it will change everything for you.

Gratitude helps us view difficult situations with greater clarity, so we can make wiser decisions. It also encourages us to think before speaking or acting, which leads to healthier communication among peers and family members. Practising gratitude allows us to focus on what we already have, rather than stressing over what we don't. It helps put things into perspective, so we understand our lives are not defined by one single moment, but rather by all the moments merged together throughout our journey towards self-fulfilment, growth, success, love, connection, peace with others, and ultimately happiness! Here are some things I am grateful for...

I am grateful for having good health and being alive.
I am grateful for this air that I breathe.
I am grateful for having a loving family.
I am grateful for my two gorgeous daughters.
I am grateful for having some truly amazing and lifelong friends.
I am grateful for loving, caring, and supportive mentors and coaches.
I am grateful for receiving a hug from a loved one.
I am grateful for having a successful career and multiple income streams.
I am grateful for having so many wonderful experiences in my life.
I am grateful for having access to the internet (the digital economy).
I am grateful for having a mobile phone.
I am grateful for having a laptop.
I am grateful for having access to a television.
I am grateful for being on a thriving journey to a successful life.

I am grateful for having discovered my purpose, values, and vision in life.

I am grateful for being on the right path to meet my future self.

I am grateful for having a nice warm home and shelter.

I am grateful for having a nice comfortable bed.

I am grateful for having access to food and water.

I am grateful for the clothes that I wear.

I am grateful for designing my own future of happiness and fulfilment.

I am grateful for being educated with digital tools & technology.

I am grateful for having a positive growth mindset.

I am grateful for the communities that are aligned with my values.

I am grateful for being educated to secure financial freedom for my family.

I am grateful for travelling and exploring this wonderful planet earth.

I am grateful for the National Health Service.

I am grateful for medical science.

I am grateful for all of the inspiring charities and fundraising events.

I am grateful for my accountability partners.

I am grateful for music.

I am grateful for public transportation.

I am grateful for shops and the retail industry.

I am grateful for my mobility and being able to go for walks.

I am grateful for motorcycles and motorsport.

I am grateful for having my own reliable car.

I am grateful for public events to entertain myself and my family.

I am grateful for living close to lovely sandy beaches.

I am grateful for publishing this book.

I am so very grateful.

What are you grateful for?...

The thing I'm most grateful for is my health. That's why it's at the top of my gratitude list. The other items in the list are not in order, but for me, health is just so important. As I'm writing this book, I have just been diagnosed with a genetic condition known as Beta Thalassaemia, which affects the blood. I never knew I was a carrier of this condition until recently, and it made me realise that our bodies are so delicate and that life is extremely precious. I will now require lifelong monitoring and treatment until the day I die.

Please remind each other of how fragile we are as humans and that we should not take anything for granted. Look after one another, in every way you can. Be the change you want to see in the world.

"Gratitude is the healthiest of all human emotions. The more you express gratitude for what you have, the more likely you will have even more to express gratitude for." – Zig Ziglar

Strategy #20 - Focus on you…Stop people-pleasing

People pleasing versus those in alignment with their authentic selves is another passionate topic for me. So, at the core of people pleasing are the belief systems. See if you can notice the difference.

I am not good enough, I am unlovable. Because of this I'm addicted to external validation, looking for love outside of myself. I have low self-esteem, and I don't really appreciate or like myself. Therefore, because of this, it's easy for me to attract takers and abusers for relationships. I will over give to others, that's how I get my validation. I will bend over backwards, and it's about my needs being last and your needs being first. I feel comfortable that way. I don't know how to set boundaries. I don't even know what my needs, values, morals are or if I do, I don't have to assert them. I can't say no and I worry about other people's opinions. I will bend to make you define me, make you like me. I probably have some kind of unhealed past trauma going on.

Whereas someone that's in alignment with their authentic self and focuses on their inner being, has the following belief systems; I am good enough, I am lovable. I have a secure sense of self, inner validation, and high self-esteem. I'll give to others, but I won't over give. It's about give and take and I'll work on compromising my relationships. I consider my needs and I'll also consider your needs, but I'll work on a compromise if those come into conflict. I have an awareness of boundaries and standards. I can say no and I will be assertive if you are mistreating me in any way. I don't really have anxiety about other people's opinions. I know that other people always have opinions, and it doesn't really matter. It's about how much I like myself, how much I value myself, how much I appreciate myself. You might like me or you might not…who cares…I like me. I have minimal past trauma, or I'm healing or have healed from that past trauma.

Can you now get a sense for the type of person you can be? Don't allow yourself to be manipulated or taken advantage of. You owe it to yourself to give yourself the maximum amount of self-love and respect that you deserve. Focus on you. You are your greatest asset.

"I used to think that the worst thing in life was to end up alone. It's not. The worst thing in life is to end up with people who make you feel alone."
— Robbin Williams

Strategy #21 - Healing triggers

I'll take you on a journey of the trigger from unhealed to healed. Let's say for example a child had abandonment in their childhood, maybe their mother or their father were neglectful, or were not fully there for them consistently, providing a stable nurturing environment - just like I experienced with my father not being there for me the day I was born and ever since.

This child would have an abandonment wound around neglect, abandonment or rejection, and so they go forward in their life with this abandonment wound, which would be triggered throughout their life. They've got an anxious attachment relationship style because of this fear of abandonment, and they will be subconsciously attracted to the very people that will abandon them. And what happens is when this person distances themselves or is unavailable, the old pain of neglect or abandonment is triggered, as well as cortisone, adrenaline from the stress response in the moment. So that is how a trigger is formed and kind of re-triggered through life. When someone doesn't heal those triggers, they may chase love, and may say; 'come back, come back and heal my abandonment. Come back and make me feel soothed again, don't abandon me.' I guess this is what I experienced in my family and intimate relationships.

These people will either chase love or they will distract themselves via addictions from their triggers. Instead of dealing with all of this old pain, the cortisone, the adrenaline, the old neglect; they will go binge eat, consume alcohol, gamble, get on social media or carry out their relevant addictions to distract from this trigger. This can just keep repeating and the person never heals their triggers.

However, to heal your trigger you must take responsibility for the trigger within you. It comes from your childhood, and you have to soothe it, and take responsibility for it in a very self-compassionate way. Therefore, the next time you get triggered, instead of chasing your addiction and being distracted from the pain, or chasing love, you must heal your trigger in the moment. You must regulate your nervous system and regulate all this pain from anxiety to calmness, from fear to love, and as you keep doing that, as you keep healing your triggers in the moment, what eventually will happen is that the wound will eventually disappear, and you will develop new belief systems.

You will start to believe that you are emotionally available to yourself. You are okay with rejection and solitude. You are very lovable and choose emotionally available people. So, now you've got these belief systems, you're going to be manifesting the life you want from this basis. You don't have that old fear of love that will leave you, that you need someone else to make you feel better. It's not easy to develop this mindset, but with patience, it will come.

Strategy #22 - Anxiety solutions

I want to share a little bit about what I discovered in managing anxiety. I shall take you through two different ways of approaching this. Just remember that anxiety is a normal emotion that we have but what's more important is how you manage and cope with it.

"People tend to dwell more on negative things than on good things. So the mind then becomes obsessed with negative things, with judgements, guilt and anxiety produced by thoughts about the future and so on. – Eckhart Tolle

Person #1 - Somebody that suffers with anxiety

They think that they're powerless over their mind.
They think that anxiety just happens, it's something external to them.
They're just ruminating on anxious thoughts.
They're ruminating on their fears creating more and more anxiety.
They're constantly sharing with their friends negativity, fears, anxieties. I know this can help, but it only helps at the moment.
They're keeping their energy or emotion up in their head, creating more and more anxiety.
They're not writing their thoughts down.

Person #2 - Somebody that suffers with anxiety, but they're working on the solutions to heal it.

They know that they have power over their mindset, and they have power over their thoughts.
They know that thoughts create emotion and anxiety. Again, we have power over our thoughts.

They're working on practising thoughts of confidence, thoughts of calmness, thoughts of peace. They know how to regulate their nervous system.

They share with their friends the solutions to their anxiety and how they're looking to heal it, manage and cope with it.

They're looking to do more body awareness, bringing the mind energy down into the body, via breathwork, yoga, stretching, and heart meditations.

They know that it's beneficial to write down their fears, challenge their fears, turn their fears into love.

Strategy #23 – Therapy

You're probably already saying that you don't want to commit to any professional support, such as therapy. I get it, I was the very same for many years. My stubbornness and resistance kicked in every time it was suggested to me by my doctor. However, I eventually faced my fear of not knowing what was on the other side of devoting time to a professional therapy program.

So, I committed to therapy with a lovely organisation known as Steps 2 wellbeing. They really looked after me and provided me with the support I needed. I had eight one-hour sessions with them, and it was free. Most importantly, it was highly confidential in a non-judgemental safe space.

During one of my sessions, the therapist played a video for me that she thought was very relevant to the moment. This YouTube video was called, "I had a black dog. His name was Depression." When I watched it, I resonated massively with this video. It was a real eye-opener for me that I was carrying this big black dog with me everywhere I went. My black dog was so big all the time and it controlled my life. It was time to accept and embrace the dog, put a lead on it and take back control of my life. I've come to terms with the fact that I will never be able to get rid of this dog.

Throughout my sessions, we referred to the snowball effect and the black dog video and how I was going to embrace my black dog, 'Rej' (from the word rejection). I came to realise that there was conflict in myself. If people didn't accept me for who I was, it didn't matter. I accepted myself.

I have now put 'Rej' on a lead. He takes me for lovely walks to calm me down and to control my emotions.

Don't be afraid to reach out for support and don't procrastinate about seeking professional help. There are so many great organisations out there that can give you the support you need. You're not on your own. You have your own 'Rej'.

Strategy #24 - Read and listen to books

As you know, reading books and listening to audiobooks are great tools for personal growth, particularly around the topic of self-help. Here are some of the audiobooks that have helped me work on myself, overcome toxic relationships, become a stronger person, and ultimately design the new life of my dreams.

'Whole Again' by Jackson MacKenzie

This book [5] is ideal if you're looking to overcome your fear of rejection. It addresses and provides crucial guidance on topics and conditions like complex PTSD, narcissistic abuse, avoidant personality disorder, codependency, core wounding, toxic shame, borderline personality disorder, and so many more.

Whole Again offers hope and multiple strategies to anyone who has survived a toxic relationship just like I have. It's also for anyone suffering the effects of a breakup involving lying, cheating, and other forms of abuse…to release old wounds and safely let the love back inside where it belongs.

For me, this book was a real eye-opener and wake-up call. As I listened to it, all I kept hearing to myself was "Yep…Yep…oh my god that's me". That's because I resonate with so much Jackson talks about. It's like hearing certain parts of my life being repeated to me.

This book has helped me discover so much about myself and other people. It has made me ask so many questions that I didn't even know existed in my life.

Have I been playing the victim role to the world this whole time?

Have I been codependent this whole time?
Have I been suffering from BPD (Borderline Personality Disorder) this whole time?
Have I been seeking external validation and approval from others?
Have I been living with a wounded inner world?
Has my BPD protective self been hiding my true identity?
Have I been living a life of self-sabotage?
Was I really in a Cluster B personality disorder relationship for nearly six years?

This book has taught me so many things, not just about myself, but how I approach relationships, people, and life in general. It has taught me how to set healthy boundaries so I can set myself free, free from playing the victim, and take on more responsibilities in my life. This is achieved through mindfulness practices, where I get to truly heal my inner world and the wounds that I have been carrying for so long.

I am not a bad person, and my intention is to restore a healthy relationship with myself and to discover my true identity…You can do the very same. It's not too late.

We now get to deconstruct our protective-self and change the wavelength (frequency) that we're tuned into…we get to reactivate our own source of unconditional love, so we no longer need to seek it from others…we get to remove the co-dependency mask that we've been wearing for all these years.
We get to be the change we want to see in the world.

Thank you very much Jackson for this powerful and insightful book.

'The Secret' and 'The Power' by Rhonda Byrne

The Secret [6] and The Power [7] are closely linked. The Secret revealed the law of attraction and in The Power, Rhonda reveals the greatest power in the universe: The Power to have anything you want. With these books, you will begin to understand that all it takes is just one thing to change your relationships (toxic and broken relationships), wealth, health, happiness and your entire life.

The life of your dreams has always been closer to you than you realised, because the power to have everything good in your life, is inside you. To create anything, to change anything, all it takes is just one thing... The Power.

Choose love and you shall receive love. The law of attraction is responding to your thoughts and feelings. Love is the positive force of life. Whatever you give out in your life is what you receive in. Give positivity, and you shall receive positivity. Give negativity, and you shall receive negativity.

Your thoughts and words can't do anything for you without your feelings.

Love is the highest feeling and frequency you can have and then in descending order comes, Gratitude, Joy, Passion, Excitement, Enthusiasm, Hope, Satisfaction.

These are the good feelings and frequencies. Then comes bad feelings and frequencies, Boredom, Irritation, Disappointment, Worry, Criticism, Anger, Hate, Envy, Guilt, Despair, Fear.

Simply by feeling good, all of that love must come back to you. Good feelings mean you're feeling happy, and joyful. Feeling good is what brings a really good life…a happy life. Love is the source of all good feelings.

You are the director of your life movie…

Everything is based on how you feel. Whatever you want is because it will make you feel good. Whatever you don't want will make you feel bad. Good feelings bring what you do want, which bring you more good feelings, and the cycle continues.

You have to be happy first to receive happy things. Amplify your love and good feelings by thinking of everything you love. Every day is an opportunity for a new life.

Imagine and feel love for what you want.
Imagine if you had the perfect body, you always dreamed of…
Imagine if you were fit and healthy…
Imagine if you were in the happiest, loving relationship with your soulmate…
Imagine if you had the best relationship with everyone in your family…
Imagine if you were living in your dream home with your dream car…
Imagine if you had so many great friends around the world who appreciate you…
Imagine if you had your dream job or business…
Imagine if you were financially secure and independent…
Imagine if you never had to worry about paying your bills ever again…
Imagine if you had everything you ever wanted…
Imagine if you could be the person you were born to be…
Imagine if you could do everything that you want to do in life…
Imagine if you were living your future self-right now…

You have to feel the things you want and feel the love for everything you desire. Do this for seven minutes a day until you truly feel you have what you want. Do it until you know your desire belongs to you. Move into a new world with everything you want. The purpose of your life is to love.

As far as the law of attraction is concerned, there is only one person in the world…you. Turn away from the things you don't love and don't give them any feeling as they are fine as they are. They have no place in your life. Instead say YES!

Don't listen to anyone who says you're not worthy or that you have to justify yourself, just like I did. The force of love says give love for whatever you want, have, or be…you are worthy and deserving just as you are. You are good enough…You are an unlimited being…You can have whatever you want…You can be anything you want to be…You can do anything you want to do…You have to tell your story…start telling it and the law of attraction must ensure you receive it. Fall in love with life…there is no limit to the amount of love you can feel. When you fall in love with life, every limitation disappears. You will become unlimited, unstoppable, and invincible.

How?

You adore everything about life with all your heart.

Whatever you're doing, wherever you are, look for cafes, cars, shops you love. Look for everything you love in people or nature. See what you love, feel what you love. Do what you love to do. When you do all this, you truly feel love.
Say I love…and all the things you love. I love…I love…I love…etc. write it out in a list. List all of the things you love…everything.

Your job is to love as much as possible every single day and turn away from the things you don't love. Love is the master key that opens the gates of happiness.

Next in these books by Rhonda, we come onto gratitude, which I covered in strategy #19. Gratitude is the great multiplier.
It begins with two simple words…Thank you. Gratitude is the bridge from negative feelings to an abundant feeling of love. There are three ways to use gratitude.

Be grateful for the past (what you have already received)
Be grateful for the present (what you're receiving now)
Be grateful for the future (what you want to receive).
The more gratitude you give, the more love you give, and the more love you give, the more you receive. If there is a delay in receiving what you want, it's only because you're not on the same feeling frequencies that you desire. The purpose of your life is joy. The greatest joy in life is giving and there is only one thing you can give…your love, your positivity, your gratitude. Unless you give, you're always going to struggle to survive. When you give love, you are fulfilling the purpose of your life.

Thank you very much Rhonda for these powerful and insightful books.

'The Body Keeps The Score (Mind, Brain and Body in the Transformation of Trauma)' by Bessel Van Der Kolk

This book [8] has been described as the trauma bible, and it explores in detail how trauma affects the body and mind. Bessel describes innovative treatments for recovery.
The effects of trauma can be devastating for sufferers, their families, and future generations. Here one of the world's experts on traumatic

stress offers a bold new paradigm for treatment, moving away from standard talking and drug therapies and towards an alternative approach that heals mind, brain, and body.

What distinguishes 'The Body Keeps the Score' is that the author, Bessel Van Der Kolk, is both a scientific researcher with a long history of measuring the effect of trauma on brain function, memory, and treatment outcomes, and an active therapist who keeps learning from his patients what benefits them most. This makes for a deeply personal, analytic, and highly readable (not to mention incredibly moving) approach to the topic of trauma recovery.

Having suffered from PTSD myself, it has given me more awareness in so many areas of my life.

Thank you very much Bessel for this powerful and insightful book.

Strategy #25 - New boundaries and standards

As Jackson alluded to in his book, *'Whole Again,'* and as I have mentioned a few times in this book, particularly in chapters seven and eight, it is so important to adapt and pivot with new personal boundaries, when faced with emotional trauma. This is so we create a higher set of standards for ourselves. Think of this as our own personal policy or ground rules - the rules that we apply and live by, and where we are in integrity with our values and beliefs all of the time.

The problem for me is that I failed to act when people showed me their true colours. It's okay to see the good in people, but when someone tells you who they are, it's a good idea to listen. When someone shows you who they are, you should really be paying attention. That's where I went wrong. Like when Lauren told me that she was selfish and dead inside, I didn't react to those red flags and step back, when ultimately, I should have.

How could I have ever detected that my soulmate had another side to her? The idealisation was too perfect. But when I look back now, I realise that was just not true. There were many moments of judgement, criticism, betrayal and manipulation. Some of these occurred quite early on in our relationship, but instead of trusting myself, I ignored these issues and tried to keep the peace, to just be nice and forget about it. I lost count of how many chances I gave her to respect me and love me for who I was. Then I felt shocked, hurt, and betrayed when I saw her for who she really was. I was so distracted with my own fantasies, hopes and dreams, that I ignored reality. I don't mean any of this as victim blaming, the fault of abuse goes on the abuser.

Boundaries are actually a by-product of us liking ourselves. When we care about that person close to us, we want what's best for that person. We stand up for ourselves to protect our needs. When the relationship with Lauren was deteriorating, I remember saying that I was setting new boundaries. However, I found myself going back to old habits…letting her back into my life…giving her chance after chance. I was not creating new boundaries, but instead, I was giving her permission to manipulate and control me. I allowed her to walk all over me. Maybe it's because I was a codependent, who was renowned for avoiding new boundaries.

But because of the way society has programmed us as humans, not all of us are nice. Therefore, we have to protect ourselves. Because I skipped that step, my body started telling me that something was wrong. When Lauren left me in March 2023 for the final time, I became physically fatigued and felt completely wiped out. It felt like all of my energy was sapped and drained from my body, and I was struggling to survive. Also at this point, I was now consciously more aware of the red flags and warning signs to watch out for in other people. However, my body was now starting to react to the emotional trauma. This is something I never ever want to experience again and is something I won't allow to happen again because of my heightened senses of red flags and alarm bells. I have set new triggers and outliers to detect disrespect, lack of trust, and lack of love towards myself and my family.

When we truly take care of ourselves, there is no need for resentment. It's no longer required. We no longer require anger to avoid a toxic person. Releasing this anger and resentment allows the body to release that tension and tightness that has been building up. This is why my body felt so stiff and rigid for so long. I had never allowed myself to be free from resentment. The same could be said when I had to deal with so many job losses in the corporate world.

I told myself that I wouldn't keep putting myself in that same vulnerable position anymore, which is why I am focusing so much of my time and effort on diversification, instead of relying on one stream of income. So, when one income source stops for any reason, there is still financial protection through other sources of income. For me, this is the new way of living…this is modern wealthy.

I have now implemented a new set of boundaries that are more aligned with who I really am. These boundaries and degrees of self-respect no longer take me out of integrity with who I truly am - my true authentic self. I no longer see myself as the hero trying to save everyone from their own personal traumas. I am a hero saving myself.

In the past, I would have always given in. But now, I just can't do it anymore. Over the years I exhausted all my energy trying to protect Lauren and meet all of her needs. Even now, I genuinely want her to be happy, but I cannot save everyone I see going through similar relationship, family or career problems. I can give good solid advice, but I can't be their superhero. I know this may sound like it's contradicting my ethos, but I want to help other people, millions of people in fact, if they are committed to working on themselves and want to include me in that process.

The number one priority in my life is looking after myself and no longer being codependent. I value myself and I give myself unconditional love. I have restored my connection with love, self-love and self-respect. I no longer require external validation, instead, I've shifted my focus internally and I've committed to making healthier, smarter decisions in my life. It's also about deconstructing my protective self, at the same time as discarding all core wounds that have never served me. This is about removing all the masks I've been wearing for so many years, which have been holding me back, preventing me from being my true authentic self.

These days, I do not commit to a new relationship until I am one hundred percent happy, and confident with the other person. This is in every way, including their values and their intentions. I shall connect with that person based on who they are at that moment, not who I want them to be. I shall never end up in a cluster B relationship ever again. These simply go against my own values and beliefs. I seek qualities such as stability, security, respect, love, trust, authenticity, communication and deep connection. I have discovered my true identity with my new lifetime boundaries, and I am manifesting abundance, wealth, health, love, success, and happiness.

What new boundaries are you creating for yourself? This would be a great opportunity for you to assess your values, and to gain clarity on your tolerances and boundaries in your life.

Strategy #26 - Every roadmap needs traffic lights

As I write this, I feel incredibly vulnerable, but in a good way. I feel like I am finally seeing my worth. Like so many, I just want to feel loved. I want to belong. But with a shaky self-esteem, this was never going to be easy. Looking for love and feeling deserving of love are not the same things.

It was inevitable that I had no self-love and I was going to get hurt, because I craved love from someone else, more than I was willing to love myself. So many people do, even if they don't admit it.

I had no barriers, no form of defence to protect myself. However, having learned the biggest lesson in life, I have now implemented my own life risk-assessment, where I have established control measures in all areas of my life. This now gives me the protection that I deserve.

The first thing I would do is to design my very own, 'Fran's mindmap of limitations'.

These are virtual zones that I visualise in my mind and they each serve a very distinct purpose. They are like a traffic light system - a green zone, an amber zone and a red zone, and they each have a unique role to play. I have structured it this way because I want to be very clear with my decisions. This covers people's behaviour towards me, how they make me feel and what energy they have. Not only that, but it also takes into account how I respond to the people around me. In other words, what are my reactions to the people in my space? Depending on the situation, and how they make me feel, then I would classify the situation and allow protections to come into place. So, it really is a control strategy for my own feelings.

Green means "Fran, you're good to go!"

The green zone is where I'm naturally based, it's my default. This is where I'm grounded and feel like my authentic self. It is where I find my own and other people's behaviours, core values and belief systems 'Acceptable'. I'll now share with you what I expect to find and experience in this space in no particular order.

Motivation
Love
Care
Pride
Gratitude
Support
Respect
Positive Attitude
Kind
Generosity
Empathy
Compassion
Sympathy
Loyalty
Belief
Hope
Ambition
Connection
Transformation
Courage
Self-Love
Brave
Open-Mindedness
Adventure
Authenticity

Power
Unstoppable
Joy
Happiness
Worthiness
Leadership
Considerate
High Frequency Energy
Growth Mindset
Calm
Inclusion
Peace
Abundance
Freedom
Honesty
Integrity
Value
Safe
Secure
Self-Reliability
Relaxed
Acknowledgement
Trust

Amber means "Fran, Caution Ahead!"

The amber zone is a very thin area between the green and red zones. It is what I call my 'Limitation Line'. The best way I can describe this is referring to it as my testing experience of systems. Every vehicle system has a minimum and maximum limit. This is to protect that system from failure. So, whenever the system comes out of limits, an outlier is triggered and provides an amber or yellow caution sign and sound to indicate that it's now operating outside its normal operating envelope...In other words, 'Caution', just like you see on your car dashboard.

So, in simple terms, this is what I'm now applying in my life. Whenever I experience something that's outside my normal, 'Green' envelope, my nervous system goes into this amber zone, and depending on the severity and frequency of the event, it may go into the red zone, which means shutdown and disconnect from that person or environment. If I felt everything was safe, it would drop back into the green zone again, meaning carry on as normal with this person or this environment. However, this is dependent on the situation, I now have a system, a strategy in place to protect myself and my nervous system. This is a subjective method, but it is a control mechanism to protect my inner self from external factors. I no longer allow myself to be bullied, manipulated, or controlled in any way, by anybody. It's about having complete awareness of the situation you're in, how you feel, and what your emotions and your body are telling you. Is this a system that would work for you? Develop your mindmap of limitations (green, amber, and red zones) for your new life and see how much more protected and resilient your nervous system becomes.

Red means "WTF are you doing Fran?!"

The red zone is where I find people's behaviour 'Unacceptable' and I start to shut-down on people. I have a zero-tolerance policy in this area. Having created new boundaries for myself, I call this the 'Red Flag Zone' and it's where I do not want to find myself in with people. You may resonate with a lot of the terms I'll share with you, but these are the behaviours that are non-negotiable in my life:
Manipulation
Control
Bullying

Judgement
Patronising
Walk all over me
Take advantage of me
Unfaithful to me
Narcissistic trauma
Lies and deceit
Betrayal
Critical
Abusive
Stab me in the back
Call the police on me
Play the victim game
Rude
Immature
Underestimate me
Negative mindset
Jealousy
Disrespect
Mind games
Hot and cold
Not believe in me
Read my text messages
Bitch about me
Block me on socials
Unsupportive
Self-centred
Self-obsessed
Unreliable
Rejection
Abandonment
Take me for granted
Low frequency energy

Strategy #27 - Find your tribe

Another great technique that I have found to help with the fear of rejection, abandonment and betrayal is to surround yourself with those you want to become.

Listen to motivational speakers and entrepreneurs. This can either be through their podcasts, YouTube channels, or social media platforms. These are people who have been in similar situations, been kicked to the ground by society and lost everything but have somehow found the strength within to pick themselves up and keep fighting. They are warriors, who have certainly inspired me to keep moving forward. Here are a few that I would highly recommend you follow and listen to on YouTube and other social media channels.

You could even book tickets to some of their live events around the world.

Tony Robbins
Jim Rohn
Robert Kiyosaki
Grant Cardone
Dean Graziosi
Mel Robbins
Tim Ferriss
Warren Buffett
Steve Bartlett
David Goggins

I have now created a new habit, and I have integrated this into my morning routine (the morning miracle). I listen to a motivational speaker for about ten to twenty minutes at the start of each day. This is so I am empowered, inspired and motivated to create the maximum each day. I want to be full of energy, excitement and motivation to feel unstoppable. This sets me up perfectly for whatever I face each day. It's like my fuel to keep that fire burning inside of me. Why not give it a go? You will find your fire starter.

Strategy #28 - Fran's bad to good valve

It's not as crazy as it sounds...let me explain!

I'm sure like me, you have all of these voices (nerds) in your head that seem to control your life. You probably spend many minutes, even hours in the day having conversations with yourself. This is perfectly normal...you are human.

Looking back over my life, particularly around the time I was in a toxic relationship, I can remember a number of occasions when I would go for a walk in the morning before I started my workday. This is no word of a lie, I would spend the entire time in a dialogue with myself and my ex-partner. Yes, I would have a conversation with her in my own head. I would do this on the full length of my walk, which was about six kilometres. I would have no recollection of the journey, what I saw, who walked past me...Nothing...Crazy I know.

Since then, I have been working on my own techniques to overcome this battle. One method I've started using is what I call my bad to good valve... Let me explain. If good, happy and positive emotions are flowing within me, then I would let them flow, and I would see positive results in my life. Everything would be wonderful.

If bad, and negative emotions are flowing within me, then I would attract more negativity into my life, and this is something I do not want anymore. Therefore, I would need to do something to change this.

A solution for me when I experience myself dealing with one of my negative noisy nerds, is that I would activate a valve in my mind (like a bypass valve) and channel that energy from the negative side over to the positive side of my mind. In other words, if I was having a dialogue in my head with Lauren, I would very quickly and consciously deflect that flow into something positive, like the opportunities within my new and exciting vision, or this new and exciting income stream that I'm working on. Does that make sense?

The key is having the awareness to catch yourself. For me, I would say to myself "switch the valve", and that would immediately bring me into the conscious state of switching from my bad to good valve, removing those negative thoughts and converting them into something magical, like my vision, or gratitude.

Next time you catch yourself having a fight with your nerds, I want you to try and change the direction of flow. In other words, deflect that negative thought, so it converts into a new and exciting positive one that fills you with joy and happiness.

Strategy #29 - Fran's rejection journey

Inspired by Jia Jiang's book, "Rejection-Proof" [9], I committed to embark on my own journey of facing rejection head-on. Jia puts it into perspective that not all, 'No' responses are negative and devastating. In fact, they can lead to new opportunities and possibilities.

I decided to go for it, put myself in the face of rejection and take myself on my own rejection journey. I didn't commit to the same level of one hundred days of rejection as Jia did. I thought I would start slow and eventually integrate this into my life as a new habit. However, I want to share with you the types of environments that I put myself into to face rejection.

Everyone experiences rejections countless times over the course of their lifetime, I get that. Ultimately, few if any of these rejections will prove to be life-threatening, yet nearly every one of these rejections makes us feel bad. However, they also offer us an opportunity to grow, challenge ourselves, and help to overcome the fear and insecurities that block us from unleashing our full potential. Of course, one of the greatest lessons of my journey was that any rejection can have a hidden upside or new possibilities. I really encourage you to use this experience of rejection to strengthen and motivate your career, your family life, and your relationships...convert rejection into your own personal fuel and re-ignite your life. This shall prove your worth.

My first rejection attempt was on my way to Bournemouth airport. This was just before I bought a new car, and I got a taxi from work to the airport. This was only about a twenty-minute drive, so it wasn't too far to travel. I had planned to do this before my trip, so I was a nervous wreck in the taxi as I was about to ask the driver for a big favour. I was doing everything possible to stay calm. I was chatting with the driver, so I could build up our relationship and establish a rapport. This moment of truth was upon me. We were entering the airport and I now had to commit. So here I went...I somehow managed to build up enough courage to ask the driver for a deal on the taxi fare. I begged him to offer me a reduced fare. Well maybe I didn't beg, but whatever I did, he unfortunately couldn't do me a deal. Before I said goodbye, I felt a sense of pride inside of me...even though the driver had said no, it was the fact that I simply made the request. I had been building up my emotions and anxiety for something quite small. The worst he could say was no, and that's what I got. As humans, we tend to overthink and over-analyse things more than we need to. When I actually think about it, my request was a reduced fare. However, I had built up my mind to what I thought was so much scarier than that, when in fact it was so minor.

My second rejection attempt was again in an airport. This time it was in Dublin airport coming back to Bournemouth. However, this time it was in the fast-food chain Burger King, but with a slight twist. This was the time of the British King's coronation. So, what I decided to do was ask the guy behind the counter if he could make me a special "Coronation Burger". I just had to do it. Again, like the first time, my nerves and anxiety built up and I was far from relaxed doing it. This was now really taking me out of my comfort zone, which scared me. So I looked at the menu above his head, and of course, I could not see a coronation burger on the menu. Instead, I politely asked, "I don't suppose you do a coronation burger?"

The guy looked at me with such a confused face. He had no idea what I was talking about. I repeated myself, but he was not on the same page as me. He was certainly not going to make me a special burger, let alone a king's coronation burger. So instead of trying any further with my outrageous request, I asked if I could have a cup of tea. I wasn't even hungry. I just wanted to make that request so I could get rejected. I walked away with my tea chuckling away to myself. In a weird way, I felt happy. Not because of not getting my special coronation burger, but because I could actually push myself to do these ridiculous requests.

This is a process that definitely helps me overcome my limiting beliefs and one that stretches me like an elastic band in facing my fear of rejection. I didn't do many of these to begin with, but it's great practice to prepare yourself for the inevitable 'No', and what opportunities may come from each experience.

Give it a try…I'm still doing it…Happy rejection journey!

Strategy #30 - Fran's V-model (Vision strategy)

Drum roll please...Here we are at what I believe to be the most exciting strategy of all. One thing I learned when developing systems in the engineering world, was that there was a process in place known as the "System Engineering V-Model" that clearly defined how to verify and validate customer requirements.

The importance of the System V-Model when designing and developing new features cannot be overstated. This model allows engineers to clearly define customer requirements, and how these must be verified and validated at each stage of the development process. Let's take a closer look at this.

On the left-hand side of the "V", the customer's high-level requirements must be defined. This is what the customer or client wants in terms of a new feature, system, or even a full vehicle that they want to put out into the marketplace. This then enables program managers and engineers to develop the next phase, which is the system-level requirements, followed by component level requirements. This gives the engineers the component hardware and software 'shopping basket' they need. It provides clarity on the ingredients needed to create this new feature, system, or vehicle.

At this point, we now move to the right-hand side of the "V" for verification and validation. This is where my testing experience comes into play. As a test and development engineer, I would verify and validate various systems that had already been through the requirements definition phase.

The component-level verification is perhaps the most important part of this process. Once the components are defined, engineers can then use this knowledge to effectively verify that all customer requirements are met. These tests are usually carried out in HiL rigs (Hardware-in-the-Loop) and as an example, components like the engine control unit (ECU) are tested in this way.

System-level verification follows shortly after component verification. Engineers, like me, make sure that everything at the system level works as it should, with respect to customer requirements. This is verifying the functional and performance characteristics of the system. System-level testing is typically carried out in test rigs, where the configuration is bespoke to that system, such as dynamic rigs like for a full four-wheel-drive (FWD) powertrain and driveline installation, like the ones I used to test.

Finally, once both these levels are completed, full system testing can take place before the final launch into production. Typically, this is representative of the vehicle installation. In other words, I would test a system such as the ACC (Adaptive Cruise Control), using a fully functioning camouflaged development vehicle on public roads and proving grounds or test tracks. I would work very closely with the system engineer team to ensure we met our targets. For example, the acceleration and deceleration rates and how smoothly the car performed in various driving traffic conditions. Not only that, but also ensuring the system integrated with the rest of the vehicle.

This is the validation of the customer requirements and is the final phase of the system V-model process. Through this process, companies and engineers can make sure that their new product meets customer expectations, while also meeting all of the required safety and performance standards. It also ensures accuracy throughout the entire design and development process, in order to deliver a product or service on time and within budget constraints.

I have now applied the same principle to design and develop my new life vision. I get to give myself permission to define my own V-Model vision strategy and define my own shopping basket ingredients for this new vision of mine. It's everything I get to have and be, so that I can live my best life, whilst following this same process. You can also design your vision this way as well...It's time to fill your life's shopping basket full of wonderful things.

I recommend getting a piece of paper and a pen, or if you prefer to type it out on your laptop or computer then that's fine, but now is your moment to get the clarity on your V-Model, your vision for your future.

Step 1 - Define your requirements, your vision (What/Why)

Creating a strategic vision for your life is key to your success. It is the first step in setting the direction of where you want your life to go and how you will achieve personal growth. But firstly you have to ask yourself: Why do I want this?

When crafting a vision statement, start by asking yourself why are you doing this? What do you hope to accomplish? What kind of impact do you want to make on the world around you? Once you can answer these questions, build out the details of your larger-scale goals. Start with long-term ambitions and then work backward from there, breaking down each goal into achievable steps, reverse engineering your vision to make this a reality for you and your family. Write down as much as you can and be clear about what it is you want.

What Do You Want?...What Do You Want?...What Do You Want?...

Here is a brief summary of what I want in my life:

I want to fall in love with life.

I want great physical and mental health for everyone in this world.

I want to live in a world of peace, love, freedom, connection, and abundance.

I want to live a long and healthy life, where I can live a full life.

I want to have the well-toned six-pack abs body I've always dreamed of.

I want to be full of energy and have a well-balanced nutritious diet.

I want to have the strength and fitness to run marathons.

I want to be free from alcohol, cigarettes and drugs, for the rest of my life, as they do not serve me in any way.

I want to feel happy, joyful, confident, and full of excitement every second, every day.

I want to set a good example for my family, my children and for them all to be proud of me.

I want to leave behind a generational legacy

I want my children to build their own legacy in life.

I want to spend more quality time, creating happy memories with my children, and my loved ones.

I want to have a circle of friends, a community or tribe of like-minded people who love me, respect me, trust me and appreciate me for who I am, unconditionally.

I want to do the things I'm passionate about and enjoy doing.

I want to be in a loving relationship, where my partner cares for me, supports me, adores me, loves me, respects me and trusts me unconditionally.

I want to marry the love of my life and live happily ever after together.

I want to have a thriving and successful business and career, where I'm transforming millions of lives around the world.

I want to work a four-hour work week.

I want to break free from the 9-to-5 corporate job (broken system).
I want to generate multiple streams of income on autopilot, and earn 24/7, 365 days a year.
I want to become a multi-millionaire.
I want to live a life of financial freedom and independence, being self-reliant, and self-sufficient, with long-term stability.
I want to live a life of diversification (not relying on one source of income).
I want to have wealth in abundance with a growing investment portfolio.
I want geographical freedom.
I want to break free from toxic, selfish, and negative people who are not aligned with my values.
I want to break free from all the hurt and pain that I've been carrying around with me all my life.
I want to live a life of integrity, and honesty.
I want to acknowledge and give myself self-love and self-respect.
I want to be kind to myself.
I want to maintain high personal standards and boundaries in every area of my life, so that my inner being is fully protected.
I want to travel the world and explore so much of our beautiful planet, meeting extraordinary people.
I want to contribute more to the world helping others who are in need of aid, particularly in natural disasters i.e charity organisations.
I want to invest in personal growth and personal development so that I become the best version of myself.
I want to be my authentic, powerful, loving self.
I want to be in complete control of my life, living it on my terms.
I want to be bold, brave, and courageous in going after my dreams.
I want to live a happy and fulfilled life of meaning and purpose.
I want a growth mindset where I can manage my emotions so that I feel happy, content, relaxed, with positive energy every day.
I want to be laser-focused on my vision every day.

I want to focus on self-help, self-healing, and self-discovery.
I want to live a limitless life with freedom and flexibility.
I want to feel happy and whole again.
I want to feel worthy…I am worthy of love and belonging.

Step 2 - Map your life (System Level)

Once your vision is clearly defined and you know what you want, it's now time to break this down into all the areas of your life. Next to each item you have written down, you need to mark them with what area of your life they belong to. There are four areas of your life: Wealth, Health, Self and Social.

If it's Wealth, mark it with "W"
If it's Health, mark it with "H"
If it's Self, mark it with "Se"
If it's Social, mark it with "So"

Make sure you have as many as possible in each quadrant.

<u>Wealth (W)</u> - All things financial, such as your career and your financial investments are included in this area. It's also about diving into your mindset on money and identifying any roadblocks to the flow of abundance in your life. Learning to create value in the marketplace is also important if you're serious about growing your influence and finances. This is about having money work for you, instead of you working for one single pay cheque.

I personally know what it's like to rely on one source of income and lose multiple jobs. So, I can admit that this strategy is far too risky. Do not put all of your eggs into one basket, especially during these uncertain times, it's all about diversification and creating that financial security and freedom through multiple sources of income that you or your family needs. Gain control of your financial future.

"The main reason people struggle financially is because they have spent years in school but learning nothing about money. The result is that people learn to work for money... but never learn to have money work for them" – Robert Kiyosaki, 'Rich Dad Poor Dad.'

Health (H) - Physical health is the most important aspect of life, as it can be the foundation for a person's overall well-being. When someone is physically healthy, they have more energy and vitality, which allows them to engage in activities and relationships that bring joy to their lives. Being physically fit requires a combination of exercise, nutrition and mobility.

Exercise is essential to maintain physical health. It strengthens muscles and bones, improves balance and coordination, increases endurance, and helps with weight management. Exercise also helps increase mental clarity, reduce stress levels, boost self-image, improve sleep quality and much more. There are many different types of exercise that can benefit someone's physical health such as aerobic exercises like running or swimming; strength training like weightlifting; stretching exercises like yoga; or even sports such as football or tennis. Finding an activity that you enjoy can make it easier for you to stick with it in the long run.

Nutrition plays a key role in promoting physical health. Eating foods that are rich in vitamins, minerals, fibre, and other nutrients are necessary to stay healthy. Nutritionists typically recommend eating a balanced diet composed mostly of vegetables and fruits along with some lean proteins, such as fish or poultry, as well as some whole grains such as oats. Staying away from processed foods full of sugar or salt is also recommended for optimal nutrition, since these tend to cause weight gain, while providing minimal nutritional value. Supplements such as protein shakes may be beneficial if someone has difficulty getting enough nutrients solely through food sources alone.

Finally, mobility is important for being physically healthy as well. This means having the ability to freely move without pain or discomfort from injuries or illness. We should practise proper posture when sitting for long periods of time at work or home, so our spine doesn't become misaligned over time due to poor ergonomics habits - leading to chronic pain down the road.

Additionally, engaging in regular stretching activities helps keep joints limber and reduces muscle tightness, caused by repetitive movements like typing on a computer keyboard all day long. Stretching isn't only important before exercising, regular stretch sessions have long-lasting benefits on mobility.

Self (Se) - The importance of knowing and understanding yourself emotionally is crucial to achieving strong mental well-being. Having the ability to manage your emotions and react in a healthy way can make life easier and less stressful. Self-care is the cornerstone of any mental health routine, as it helps us take care of our minds and bodies, so that they can support us through difficult times.

Self-care is not about selfishly focusing on your own needs, but rather finding a balance between taking care of your body, mind and spirit, while also tending to the needs of those around you. It's important to recognise that self-care doesn't have to be expensive or time-consuming; simple activities like journaling, meditating, or taking a walk outside are all great ways to practice self-care.

In addition to engaging in basic self-care activities, it's also important to create rituals that help centre you during moments of stress or anxiety. Whether it's reading a book or stretching for five minutes when you wake up, finding small ways throughout the day to reconnect with yourself can be powerful in managing emotions. The miracle morning routine that I previously mentioned will help with this.

It's also important to recognise when more intensive care is needed; for instance, if you are experiencing persistent feelings of sadness or hopelessness, it may be beneficial to consult a professional who can provide guidance on how best to cope with these emotions. Mental health professionals such as therapists, psychologists, psychiatrists, social workers and coaches can all offer valuable insight into what strategies work best in managing emotions and creating healthier daily habits.

Ultimately, understanding yourself at an emotional level requires continual effort and practice; however, the benefits gained from having strong mental well-being cannot be underestimated. Taking small steps each day towards better understanding your emotional state will not only help you live a healthier life but will also give you the tools necessary for navigating life's difficulties with greater ease.

Social (So) - Social life is an essential part of life that helps us to stay connected with the world and develop meaningful relationships with others. From family members to friends, acquaintances, and even strangers, socialising can be a great way to learn more about ourselves, others and the world around us.

To maintain healthy relationships with those around us, we must prioritise our social lives and make time for shared experiences. Forming real connections through conversation and mutual understanding can only happen when we invest effort into it. Taking part in activities like attending parties together or having dinner with family members helps build connections and relationships. Additionally, setting aside time for recreational activities, such as going on holiday or playing sport, can be beneficial for bringing people closer together.

Exploring hobbies and interests can also help you build deeper relationships. Participating in outdoor activities, for me, this involves motorsport track days, watching superbike racing, or going for walks with family members and friends. Furthermore, participating in events such as comedy clubs and seeing live events allows us to express our feeling of being happy, where we can have a laugh (literally!) with friends. These are things I want to do more of, as it's all about having fun in life.

Making time for fun should be a priority as it allows us to unwind from the daily stresses and live life to the fullest. Engaging in leisurely activities such as watching movies or playing sports promotes relaxation, while allowing us to regain our energy, so we are better prepared for our next challenge. Having fun not only serves as a great stress reliever, but also boosts morale, which in turn motivates us to face whatever comes our way head-on rather than shying away from it.

When all is said and done, relationships are paramount in leading a fulfilling life and prioritising socialisation is key. Life is too short not to embrace fun times spent with loved ones; take time out of your schedule each week solely for developing meaningful connections with those around you and live life without regret.

Step 3 - Life strategy (Component Level)

Now that we have identified the four quadrants of our lives, it's time to break this down even further and establish how we develop a life strategy, in order to give ourselves the best possible chance to live our best life.

So, let's look at each of these four areas. This is going to be different for each of us, but I wanted to share some examples of how we break this down into individual components. Be creative with this and don't let the fear get in your way. This is your vision, your life and you now you have the chance to overcome the fear of rejection and design the life you dream of.

What Do You Want?...What Do You Want?...What Do You Want?...

HEALTH

To have the physical body I dream of (toned muscles, six-pack abs, smooth & soft skin)

To have less than 15% body fat

To have fitness equivalent to running a marathon

To be free from deceases, viruses, infections, etc.

To be free from prescription medication (if possible)

To have sufficient and balanced vitamins for optimum performance

To have full body mobility (flexibility, strength, speed, etc.)

To have optimum hearing and eyesight

To have the optimum teeth (veneers, whitening, etc.)

To have the best personal hygiene (shower daily, moisturise, deodorant, aftershave, etc.)

To have short and clean fingernails and toenails

To have a healthy, balanced and nutritious diet (< 2,000 calories per day)

To be well hydrated and drink 2 to 3 litres of water per day

To have a smart appearance (latest quality fashion & brands)

To be free from alcohol

To be free from cigarettes

To be free from drugs or any mood-altering medication (including anti-depressants)

To have regular blood tests and health check-ups

To have a body that is completely relaxed and at peace with itself and life

WEALTH

To have the knowledge and skill set to be financially independent

To be able to support my family financially

To build a multi-million-pound property portfolio (leveraging other people's money)

To read books daily around having a money mindset

To have wealth in abundance

To be a multi-millionaire by the time I'm 50 years old

To have a minimum of 7 streams of income

To be recession-proof and have the tools to eliminate financial anxiety

To be debt-free

To have assets (investments, property, stocks, shares, high-ticket products, books)

To have digital assets (email list, website, sales funnels, socials, etc.)

To have money work for me (automated selling systems 24/7, 365 days a year)

To be able to live my life on my terms being in financial freedom

To have profitable, and successful businesses adding value to millions of people

To have my own unique business niche and host affordable luxury retreats at private and exclusive venues around the world (e.g. mental health, rejection & abandonment, adoption)

To develop my own mobile app

To be a bestselling author with all of my books
To be a keynote speaker at events around the world
To collaborate with Women's Biz Global, other entrepreneurs and leaders
To travel globally with Women's Biz Global as an ambassador

SELF

To have a healthy, focused mind
To have a positive, manifestation, and law of attraction mindset
To be and feel powerful
To truly step into my power
To be and feel authentic
To be loving towards myself and others
To fall in love with life
To truly feel happy
To truly feel at peace with myself
To truly feel relaxed and content with life
To feel free
To feel energetic
To feel alive
To feel enthusiastic
To always be working on my personal development & growth
To invest in myself
To face my fears and get the outcome I desire (My WHY is my driving force)
To align with my core values, my beliefs, my mission and my vision
To overcome my limiting beliefs
To be kind to myself
To protect myself and remain consistent with my personal boundaries
To do charity and volunteer work with Mental Health Motorbike
To support anyone who needs a Mental Health First Aider
To support the children in need in Nepal and across the world

To perform daily meditations and attend local yoga experiences

To attend spa experiences at least once a month

To manage my emotions using various tools and strategies

To embody and be living my future self now

SOCIAL

To be free from toxic people and relationships who do not serve me

To surround myself with the people I want to become (millionaires, influencers, leaders)

To have the best relationship and have more quality time with my two daughters, Faye and Sara (go shopping and travel the world together, etc.)

To have the best relationship and have more quality time with all of my family and friends

To do the things I'm passionate & enthusiastic about (motorbike track days, watching motor racing events with my loved ones, etc.)

To find new hobbies and interests that excite me

To build up my circle of friends

To be a leader to other people and guide them to live their best life

To have people follow me and be inspired and empowered by me

To always focus on things that make me happy (quality time with family & friends)

To find the love of my life who loves me for who I am, unconditionally and supports me in all of my ambitions, and goals in life

To have a long-term relationship, with marriage and more children

To live in a lovely big family home (mortgage-free mansion) with my new loving partner

To travel the world and make connections with people all over the world (e.g. networking at live events)

Step 4 - Fill your life's shopping basket

The next step is to fill your shopping basket with all of the ingredients you need for all four of these areas in your life.

ESSENTIAL INGREDIENTS - Time, commitment, dedication, hard work, energy, effort, passion, open mind, positive attitude, belief, willpower.

WEALTH INGREDIENTS - Specific to you, such as financial investment, savings, the stock market, property investment certification, digital marketing tools and technology, education platforms.

HEALTH INGREDIENTS - Specific to you, such as a weight loss program, nutrition plan.

SELF INGREDIENTS - Specific to you, be it a yoga mat, music playlist, or earbuds.

SOCIAL INGREDIENTS - Specific to you, for example event tickets, holiday tickets, social meetup or dating apps.

Step 5 - Verify your basket items

The next step is to take these ingredients and implement them in each area of your life. You then test and verify the performance at the component level. In other words, if one of your goals is to become a professional property investor, like I am, then you will need to invest in a property training program to gain the knowledge and skill set. Committing to this training is the first step on your property portfolio journey.

WEALTH PERFORMANCE - Have your wealth
weekly/monthly/quarterly targets been achieved?
HEALTH PERFORMANCE - Have your health
weekly/monthly/quarterly targets been achieved?

SELF PERFORMANCE - Have your self
weekly/monthly/quarterly targets been achieved?
SOCIAL PERFORMANCE - Have your social
weekly/monthly/quarterly targets been achieved?

Step 6 - Verify your life

The next step is to test and verify the performance at the system
level (all four areas of your life). All you need to do is score each
area of your life out of 10 and keep working on the areas that need
to get to that perfect 10.

WEALTH VERIFICATION - Does this provide a 10 out of 10
feeling for wealth?
HEALTH VERIFICATION - Does this provide a 10 out of 10
feeling for health?
SELF VERIFICATION - Does this provide a 10 out of 10 feeling
for self?
SOCIAL VERIFICATION - Does this provide a 10 out of 10
feeling for social?

Step 7 - Validate your vision

The final step in my V-Model process is to validate what you set out
to achieve in your vision statement. The journey of life
transformation begins with having a clear vision of what you want
to achieve. A vision statement is a powerful tool to help us focus
our energy on our goals and stay focused on the changes we want
to make in our lives. Through this process, we can identify the areas
that we are passionate about, set achievable objectives, and create a
plan of action to ensure we create the life we truly desire.

When it comes to setting goals and objectives, it is important to use quantifiable measures that can be tracked and measured to evaluate the progress of your life transformation. This will also allow you to adjust your strategies, according to changing conditions or unforeseen circumstances, such as a job loss or contract termination, a recession, a relationship breakdown, or even a divorce. We must adapt, pivot and be able to realign the area of our life that needs adjusting. Once the goals have been established, then it's time to create a plan of action that incorporates self-discipline, commitment and hard work.

Once the plan of action has been put into motion, it is important to carry out performance reviews at regular intervals throughout your life transformation journey, to assess whether everything is going according to plan and that you're meeting your targets. These may be weekly, monthly, or quarterly reviews.

Therefore, the final step of this process is validation – validating what you set out for yourself in your vision statement; whether it was tangible results, feelings, or life transformations. Have you taken steps towards bringing this vision of yours into reality? Are you now feeling as good as your 10/10 rating across all areas (wealth, health, self, and social)? In other words, do you have a deep sense of happiness, joy, and fulfilment in your life now? Are you living your best life?

This final stage of evaluation will show you whether your life transformation journey was successful, or if there needs to be further adjustments made to reach your desired destination. Ideally, you want all four quadrants to be balanced, meaning that your life is in perfect equilibrium. Ultimately, by engaging in this process with integrity and consistency, you should be able to arrive at your own individual version of success - living your true purpose in life, living your vision, and feeling happy across all aspects of your life.

"Your vision will become clear only when you can look into your own heart. Who looks outside, dreams; who looks inside, awakes". – Carl Yung

Strategy #31 – Your perfect day

The next tool, which I highly recommend, is to really visualise your perfect or ideal day. This is an exercise I discovered when I joined a community of like-minded entrepreneurs. This requires you to have a bit of fun and to really focus on how you would like to live your best life. Go into as much detail as possible, such as who you're with, how you feel, the time of the day and what you're doing. This is about exploring and really visualising the person you want to become. Here is an example of one of my perfect days. We will all have many of these days, but this is certainly one of mine:

Location
Luxury Beachfront five-bedroom penthouse apartment in The Palm Jumeirah, Dubai, UAE.
Private beach and waterfront lifestyle overlooking the Dubai Marina.

Who is with me
It's February.
My gorgeous partner.
My two beautiful children, Faye and Sara, are visiting from the UK for half-term.

My extended family are visiting for a few days.
Our maid.

Breakfast

My partner and I naturally wake up at about 7am, without any alarm clocks.

Faye and Sara like to lie in a bit longer until about 8:30am.

My family are sleeping in the other two guest rooms and are also up at about 8:30am.

The weather is so beautiful. The sun is shining, with no clouds and there is a slight breeze. The temperature is already about 20^0C when we wake up. It's perfect.

I get out of our comfortable king size bed that has Egyptian cotton covers. I have such a big smile on my face. I'm very happy, relaxed and content.

I have a lovely shower and put on some of my new clothes that I bought from the Dubai mall yesterday. They are a lovely Boss polo t-shirt and a pair of chino shorts.

My partner freshens up and also gets dressed in clothes she feels comfortable in. She is so happy, relaxed and full of energy and positivity. I love seeing her radiant smile. It makes me happy and joyful, knowing she is happy. She looks gorgeous.

We go into our large open-plan kitchen where we are greeted by our maid. She greets us with a big smile and she is already preparing our favourite drinks... Hot Chocolate!

It's about 9am when we are all sitting out on the balcony overlooking the private beach. Our maid has made a selection of food for us, pancakes with fresh fruit, pastries, and fresh cold orange juice. Amazing!

Morning

After breakfast, I get my laptop and bring it out onto the balcony. I check my emails, review my ad campaigns, reach out to clients, reach out to my property power team such as private investors, estate agents, builders, business partners. I simply check in on the performance of my businesses, which are fully automated and running in the background.

I spend about an hour on my laptop, and when we're all ready we all go for a lovely walk on our private beach.

The atmosphere is great. The locals are so friendly and want to say hello to us.

We then arranged to meet some friends down at the main Dubai mall, where we have such a great time looking around the shops and admiring the large fish tank.

We visit the Burj Khalifa, which is part of the mall, and we go up to the observation area, where we get a spectacular view of all of Dubai. It is stunning. Everyone absolutely loves the experience of being in the tallest building in the world (at the time), feeling full of positivity and joyful energy.

Lunch

It's about 1:30pm when we head back into the mall and grab a light bite for lunch at this little Italian place that does the best selection of salads, pastas and pizzas. This place overlooks the Burj water fountains. It's such a perfect setting. Of course, I go for one of my favourite meals…lasagne and chips. Delicious!

Afternoon

At about 3pm, the boys decide to go for a round of golf at one of the local golf courses for a couple of hours.

Using my BMW M5, I drive us out to one of the local golf courses for a round of nine holes, while the rest of my family stay in the mall and continue to do some shopping.

Late Afternoon

When we get back to the apartment just after 6pm, I do a bit more work on my laptop out onto the balcony with a large glass of diet coke, with some ice and a slice of lime.

I send some emails to my power team, leads and clients. I review the overall performance of my businesses.

Dinner / Evening

It is about 7pm when I take a nice refreshing shower and get myself ready for an evening with my family and friends.

We plan to have a few drinks at the apartment before going out for a nice meal.

We book an all-you-can-eat and drink evening brunch down near the Burj Al Arab.

It's booked for 8:30pm for four hours.

We book a couple of Ubers to bring us to the venue.

We have the most exciting evening. Everyone is laughing and having the best time of their life.

It's after 1am by the time we get back to our apartment.

My partner and family express real gratitude and we thank each other for a lovely day. They appreciate me for who I am and everything I've achieved.

I go to bed feeling very happy.

The Feeling

With this being my perfect day, the only way I can describe it would be that my life feels complete. I feel relaxed, content, full of joy, happiness and fulfilment.

Being around my loving partner, family and friends is the most important thing to me. Spending quality time with my loved ones.

It feels like I am literally living my best life. This would certainly be one of my perfect days.

What does your ideal day look like?

"All successful people, men and women are big dreamers. They imagine what their future could be, ideal in every respect, and then they work every day toward their distant vision, that goal or purpose." – Brian Tracy

CHAPTER TEN

DO YOU WANT TO LIVE YOUR NEW VISION?

Let's create the best version of you... now!

Doesn't that ideal day sound amazing. Well, we can all strive for that very lifestyle. It comes down to having the right mindset and have the belief in our own ability and that's what I want to come back to for a few minutes.

Being a people pleaser and focusing all of my attention on other people, I was so disconnected from my true self. There was no focus on me. I focused so long on the red flags and warning signs, I didn't realise I was completely distracted from my own issues. I sacrificed my own happiness and joy. So, I knew it was time to focus my attention inwards and identify all of the things that need my attention...low self-worth, fears, anxieties, feelings of rejection, or inadequacy.

When you invest in yourself and work on these uncomfortable sensations, you learn to build a better relationship with yourself, which naturally reflects in your relationship with others. You get to discover so much about yourself, what you're capable of, and what you have to offer the world. It's not your job to manage the emotions of others. It will drain the life out of you, as it did for me. When you learn you're responsible for your own emotions, you learn to become comfortable that others are responsible for their emotions too. With this mindset, you can finally relax and begin to heal. This is about self-love.

And that's exactly what happened to me. Having been through so many traumatic moments of rejection and abandonment, investing in many personal development programs, listening to self-care audiobooks, and having a new perspective on life, as well as falling in love with life and myself, I now have given myself the permission to stop people pleasing and to ultimately unleash my potential and gain the clarity to clearly define my new vision…Not just for me, but for the world.

And that is exactly what I want for you too…to unleash your full potential. Remember in strategy #24 with Rhonda's books, The Secret and The Power, I asked you to imagine the many things that you want in life, things that would make you feel happy. Well, I want you to continue visualising that, I want you to see your future self and become that person now.

Also, in strategy #31, I asked you to record and visualise your perfect or ideal day. Make sure you keep referring back to that, as it is effectively part of your "Why", the reason you want and need to change your life.

Embracing our POWER and AUTHENTICITY

Throughout my whole life, I have never chosen to be someone I'm not. I have always chosen to be me, my true authentic self. We all have an obligation to be true to ourselves. To lead a life of authenticity is not only a fulfilling and rewarding way to live, but it can also bring us closer to the people around us.

So, what does it mean to be our true authentic self? The basic definition of authenticity is the quality or state of being genuine or real. When we are living authentically, we are true to our values and beliefs – we don't pretend to be something else, to please other people or fit into societal norms. We accept who we are, even if that's different from what society wants us to be. It means showing up as ourselves, without fear of judgement or criticism – it means being honest and open in every situation.

Living an authentic life means living with intention and purpose – understanding the things that make us unique and working hard towards goals that reflect our individual passions. This kind of life requires courage, as it often means stepping outside our comfort zones and taking risks in order to follow our own path, rather than someone else's idea of success. But it also brings great rewards – stronger relationships, greater fulfilment, higher self-worth, higher self-love and more meaningful moments in life.

The benefits of leading an authentic life extend beyond just ourselves too – when people show up as their true selves, they create trust and a safe space for others to do the same. We become more connected both with those closest to us, as well as with broader communities around the world. By creating these emotional connections between individuals, we can build bridges towards a better future for everyone involved.

At its core, embracing authenticity is about allowing yourself to be seen and heard for who you truly are, flaws included, and without fear or judgement from others or yourself. It's about letting go of what society expects from you, and that's exactly who I am. You have a voice…a powerful authentic voice… and now it's time for it to be heard.

Fear of rejection?...What's that?

At this point, your mindset should be ready to face that fear of rejection, ready to face any 'NOs' that come your way and knock them out the park. However, it takes time to accept and acknowledge these feelings we have when it comes to rejection and abandonment. Here is my honest opinion of rejection and abandonment…

I firmly believe that rejection is nothing personal. It is not an attack on you personally. It is a reflection on the other person or business. For instance, let's look at relationships, rejection may not necessarily be about you, but instead be a projection of the other person's issues or problems. They simply find it easier to take it out on you than deal with their own emotions. That is my personal opinion, and when I look back now at my own experiences, I believe that to be the case.

When it comes to businesses and job losses, again it's a reflection of the performance of the business. Many of my job losses were to do with the company being in financial difficulties. It was nothing personal against me. But it was how I perceived it, I used to take it personally. Now, I have learned how to process rejection completely differently and I have managed to overcome my fear of it - and I know you can do the same. Simply follow what I have shared with you, and you shall be in a great position to conquer your fears.

Are you ready to go "All-In"?

Are you ready to transform your life?

Are you willing to give up who you have become to be who you are?

Are you ready to go "All-in" and overcome your fear of rejection, and abandonment, so that you can launch your way into a successful and joyful life, with self-love, and self-respect, whilst creating new and exciting daily and weekly habits?

Do you truly want to maximise your business, your relationships, and your life and take them to the next level?

I want to help you transform your life and accomplish everything that matters most to you.

Regardless of the situation and circumstances, all the bad things happening around you, and what challenges you face now, you've got to believe in your heart of hearts that you can do it…and what's more, I've got your back!

When you want something, don't expect it to be given to you. No, life isn't like that. Many doors will be closed in your face, just like I experienced, and still experience. But you have got to decide that you're going to be fearless, and you're going to go all in. You're going to be relentless. You don't care about the countless 'No's' you encounter; you need to continue to refuse to be denied.

I challenge you to not stop here and believe heavily in your aspirations, so you too will come to no longer fear the word 'NO', but instead, choose to welcome it. And when you want it as bad as you want to breathe, when you choose to say I'm willing to make any sacrifice, I'm willing to go through any pain, I'm willing to go through any suffering, I'm willing to go through whatever it takes, I know you won't be the one who surrenders.

So as we look at the future, we can decide that from this day forward, as I look at all the dimensions of my life, looking at myself mentally, emotionally, and spiritually, I'm going to do all I can do to develop me, to grow and get stronger, to make a contribution to life.

Is it easy? No. Is it worth it? Yes. Yes, your life is worth it.

Our biggest challenge is to look at our own lives and ask the question, how am I holding myself back? Am I being as creative as I need to be? Am I using every resource I have? Am I doing everything possible to find what I'm looking for? Am I being unstoppable? Am I being relentless?

The only thing that holds you back is the thing between your two ears, your mind. If you can increase your self-belief and see yourself doing better, you will. When life happens, we don't just sit there and feel sorry for ourselves. We've come too far to give up now. We've come too far to be negative now. We've come too far to start overthinking now. Put yourself in a position where you can't retreat, where it's do or die, sink or swim. Here's what you'll discover. You'll develop incredible swimming skills; you'll find yourself moving through the water like never before. Through the inspiration of desperation, you'll become more creative than ever before, so throw yourself into that pool of uncertainty.

See, most people go at it tentatively. They don't go all-in. But trust me, you won't get to your destination if you don't get in the car and drive. Most people won't even get in the car. If you want something, you've got to be relentless. You have to decide that you deserve this and that you're going to have it. Go get it. The spirit of resiliency, the spirit of grit and determination. It's in your DNA, it's in your blood. You need to focus on where we're going, not where we've come from and what's happening. You can be and do whatever you want, and nobody can stop you, except yourself. If you want to go somewhere different in life, you will need a new vehicle to get you there.

Life is like a grindstone…it can polish or pulverise you, depending on how you position yourself. Personally, I am done with life pulverising me and I have now positioned myself to be and feel unstoppable.

There's one side of pain - the suffering and discomfort side, but there's also another side, and that's called effort, it's called glory. It doesn't matter what happens to you. It doesn't matter how many times you've been fired or lost jobs in your career, it doesn't matter how many people haven't believed in you, just keep pushing forward until you get it. Say it, and actually mean it. Look in the mirror every day and say, 'yeah I'm proud of you, I love you, I believe in you, you can do anything you want, you are powerful'.

You've got to say:

"Yes…yes to my dreams, yes to me, yes, I can. It doesn't matter how many failures I've made; it doesn't matter how many mistakes I've endured; it doesn't matter about what I've done, I can make it."

And you've got to believe, even if there's no reason to believe, when everything appears to be going wrong, you're working on your dreams, and somebody that you love and trust decides to walk out on you, you still have to believe. When you see those things that you've been working on crumble in your face, you still have to believe. When friends who should be a source of strength and encouragement, relatives who should be there to inspire you and motivate you, tell you can't do it, you still have to believe. With no money in your pocket and not knowing how you're going to make it, you still have to believe. No matter what you're going through, as long as you still have breath in your body, as long as you're still alive, you're still in the game. Every day you wake up and you don't have a white chalk outline around your body, it's a great day.

You can't quit, you can't give up. You lose a job, get back up and find a new job, you lose a relationship, get back up and focus on YOU, if you get diagnosed with a rare condition, get back up and fight this illness, if you start a business and it doesn't work, get back up and try again. Don't stop, never quit. If you quit, you fail, and failure isn't an option. Your success and your happiness are non-negotiable.

If you do what is easy, your life will be hard, if you do what is easy, complain about your situation and your circumstances, stand around and be a volunteer victim like everybody else, you will surrender and give up on your dreams, become depressed, bitter and angry. But if you do what is hard, keep coming back again and again, show resilience, and actually do what you say you are going to do, then your life will be easy.
Are you ready to take your life to a whole new level?

Life is now…What are you waiting for?

Before I sign off, I want to share with you that I was recently told by a friend that by publishing this book I was going to embarrass myself and that I was living in fantasy land. At first, I was confused and hurt by this. Now, this feedback fuels the fire within me to succeed and show the world that I matter, you matter, we all matter. So, what if I don't inspire every single person on the planet with this book? My aim is simply to share my journey and give hope to those that are open-minded to the possibility of great things to come following traumatising experiences of rejection and abandonment.

I'm not here to solve everyone's problem. I'm here to help those that genuinely want to move forward and overcome this pain and poor mental health. I don't have all the answers, but I'll do my very best to support those who want it. This is me being my authentic self.

Thanks again for taking the time to read this book. I hope it has inspired you, motivated you, given you the hope that there is light at the end of the dark tunnel of rejection. And once outside that tunnel, your life will flourish and blossom into anything you dream.

Choose happiness and fall in love with life and yourself.

"New Life, New Opportunities, New Possibilities." -
Fran Wilson

Appendix: The rejection shopping basket checklist

A guide to achieving your vision, goals and dreams.

Success is not always an easy journey. Rejections are common, whether it be from a job application, college admissions, or even a new business venture. However, rather than letting rejections get you down and taking over your life goals and dreams, why not create your own rejection shopping basket checklist? This guide will help you stay focused on achieving your highest vision, goals and dreams, despite the inevitable rejections you may face along the way.

1) Clarity

First off, make sure that when making decisions about your life's path that you have clarity as to what your biggest vision is for yourself. It's important to understand what success looks like to you in all aspects of life: professional, personal development goals, relationships. Remember my four quadrants of life? Taking time to truly define this vision will give you strength when challenges come up. This vision will become your "Why" and is what will motivate you to keep going.

2) Set attainable goals

The second step is creating attainable goals that will help you get closer to reaching that vision. Start by breaking down larger objectives into smaller goals that are easier to reach in the short-term. Reverse engineer your vision. Research shows that when smaller objectives are achieved, it can lead to greater motivation for completing bigger tasks as well. As part of this step, set deadlines for each goal. This means you are holding yourself accountable by committing to certain dates that are non-negotiable. It also means progress can be monitored and tracked regularly.

3) Growth

Next, think of rejections as an opportunity for growth; don't let these moments define who you are or dictate if you can reach success or not. When facing rejection use it as a learning process and use it as your fuel to become stronger, so you can push through with even more determination and more fight. It's also important to remember that sometimes "no" doesn't mean "never" ... re-evaluate the situation and do things differently. Approach it from a different angle...Stay calm...stay focused, but most importantly, keep learning and growing.

4) Remain flexible

It is so important to remain flexible on your journey towards your vision, remember life has its own surprises, so just go with it. There may be obstacles and setbacks at times, but never give up on yourself. Instead, adjust plans, accordingly, adapt and pivot, so progress can still be made in some form, rather than just giving up altogether, due to external circumstances outside of your control. Success takes dedication, commitment and resilience, particularly knowing how to continue pushing forward. Even when things get difficult, it is essential for moving closer towards your vision.

5) Choose your life ingredients

When you have defined your vision, mapped out the four quadrants of your life, and specified the tools you need to create this dream lifestyle, it is now time to go shopping...this is your life shopping list, the most important shopping list of your life. On your list are all of the ingredients that you require in order to design the life you want and do not include toxicity, negativity, rejection, or abandonment. Your ingredients are all very exciting and will be unique to you, they are the ingredients that make you feel alive, happy, content and relaxed. It's time to live by your rule book for your life, on your terms...you are the author of your own story.

6) Verify and validate your new life

With your life basket full of wonderful things, you get to enrol in your own vision, and it's now time to build that dream lifestyle. Take each quadrant at a time, until your life feels more balanced. Ideally, you should be in complete equilibrium. Here are the four questions you should be asking yourself for each of the four areas of your life.

Is what I'm doing giving me a 10 out of 10 in Wealth?
Is what I'm doing giving me a 10 out of 10 in Health?
Is what I'm doing giving me a 10 out of 10 in Self?
Is what I'm doing giving me a 10 out of 10 in Social?

Only you can verify and validate this new shopping basket that you create, as only you are the master of your own destiny. By following these simple steps, you can create a rejection-proof shopping basket, which will put YOU one step closer towards your ultimate vision for yourself and your family, where you truly feel worthy.

"Be the change you wish to see in the world" – Mahatma Gandhi

EPILOGUE

I AM FRAN... WELCOME HOME

What a journey...a true hero's journey at that, one that spanned from agony to ecstasy.

Before writing this book, I spent forty years of my life with my eyes closed. I was so detached from reality, that I never opened my eyes to notice what was in front of me. Going from one rejection and abandonment experience to another, beginning with abandonment from the day I was born and losing not just one dad, but two.

Going from contract termination to contract termination in my engineering career, with no income and job security for my family. Society had programmed me to operate in an outdated and broken system, with the wrong mentality. Similarly, after experiencing relationships that no longer served me, I knew it was time to break the cycle; break free from this toxic and painful cycle, so that I could become the ultimate version of myself.

Now with new and improved boundaries, with protective outliers, such as my traffic light system, I have been able to give myself the best gift there is in this life...self-love.

Having set higher standards for myself, with zero tolerance for manipulation, and emotional abuse, I'm now living my life as authentically as I can. I feel truly happy and at peace with myself. I'm now on the path that I was always meant to be on. We are all on a journey, and we need to enjoy this life, as we only get one go at it.

Now, I am the Fran the world deserves to meet; more importantly, the Fran that I am proud to meet!

You too can meet your future-self, the highest and best version of you.
I hope this book will guide and support you on your journey too. I hope you feel inspired and empowered to remove the mask you've also perhaps been wearing your entire life. The mask that has been holding you back, so that you too can feel truly worthy and unstoppable in your pursuit for self-love.

Finally, I encourage you to do this one, solo self-love task: Write yourself a letter titled, "Today, I stand for…"

Although I'm only human and continue to remain a work in progress, when I ask myself what I stand for today, I can say with confidence and conviction that:

"I am a powerful, authentic, loving leader and I stand for growth, freedom, and transformation."

ACKNOWLEDGEMENTS

THANK YOU

Acknowledgements

I could acknowledge so many people and that would be another book in itself. However, not taking anything away from anyone else, here are just a few special people I would like to mention.

To Mum Sandra (my blossom):

Thank you so much for all of your love and support. I don't know where I'd be without you in my life. You have been there for me every second of every day, guiding and helping me through these dark times. You are a true angel, my hero, and my best friend.

To my family and siblings:

Thank you so much for all of your love and support. You have all been there for me when I needed you and I am eternally grateful. I love you all.

To Annie G, Ally H, Prue C and Women's Biz Global Team:

Thank you very much for your support in publishing this book globally. Your training programs and your professional publishing team have given me a new skill set and the confidence to successfully get my message, my story out there to inspire and empower millions of people. I am eternally grateful.

To all my friends:

Thank you very much. You have given me so much of your time to support me in every area of my life. This has helped me acknowledge what's important to me and you have given me some steps to move forward to design a new happy life. You have supported me over the years to become the best version of me. You have all empowered me and given me the courage, confidence, and belief to create the vision of my dreams. I am grateful.

To my photographer:

I must acknowledge the creator of my book front cover image. My experience of his photography is simply incredible. He was very supportive and listened to everything I requested. He was very accommodating, very professional, and he went above and beyond to not only give me world-class photos but an unforgettable experience. His work is so unique and very creative. The book cover is entirely his work and to this day, I still don't know how he did it. He has such a creative and innovative mind, which compliments his technical photo editing skills. He is truly inspiring. I'm already super excited to be working with him soon on my next photoshoot and project. I have no reason to find anyone else. He is a joy to work with and is such a great person to be around. Thank you.

proheadshots.uk

Resources:

References

Reference 1, page 16: U.S. Department of Health and Human Services.

https://www.usa.gov/agencies/u-s-department-of-health-and-human-services

Reference 2, page 60: Priory Group.

https://www.priorygroup.com/blog/40-of-men-wont-talk-to-anyone-about-their-mental-health

Reference 3, page 165: ISPA Repository.

https://repositorio.ispa.pt/bitstream/10400.12/3364/1/IJSP_998-1009.pdf

---

Books

Book 1: *Whole Again* by Jackson MacKenzie

Book 2: *The Secret* by Rhonda Byrne

Book 3: *The Power* by Rhonda Byrne

Book 4: *The Body Keeps The Score* by Bessel van der Kolk

Book 5: *Rejection-Proof* by Jia Jiang

ABOUT THE AUTHOR

Fran Wilson is an author, speaker, authentic entrepreneur, test engineer, professional property investor and loving leader. At the core of his ethos stands a free spirit and a transformational mindset. Born in England and raised in Ireland, Fran was pulled back to the UK in his early 20s, to pursue his career and passion in motorsport. With a Master of Science Degree in Automotive and Motorsport Engineering (MSc), Fran has built over two decades of experience as a high-performance test and development engineer. Dedicated to engineering, Fran is an innovative engineer, specialising in prototype products, including powertrain systems, chassis systems and simulators, in both the automotive and aerospace industries. Fran feels very proud to have worked on the Mercedes AMG ONE 'hypercar', which has the Formula One hybrid powertrain developed for public roads. As a debut author, Fran is passionate about bringing his book to life, after signing with one of Australia's independent publishing houses, Women's Biz Global. Fran's mission is to support people with life transformation. He is an advocate for supporting mental health, rejection, abandonment, personal growth and development. He wants his book to inspire people to live their best life. Fran is also a mental health first aider. Fran is a family man. He has two teenage daughters, three adopted siblings and three biological siblings. You will likely spot Fran at motorcycle track days, attending Formula One and Superbikes racing events, socialising with friends and family. He wants to surround himself with the people he wants to become, so he is passionate about attending personal development and business networking events all around the world with like-minded people.

fran-wilson.com

Milton Keynes UK
Ingram Content Group UK Ltd.
UKHW031848251024
2346UKWH00001B/45